CASES IN
FINANCIAL
MANAGEMENT
FIRST CANADIAN EDITION

CASES IN
FINANCIAL
MANAGEMENT
FIRST CANADIAN EDITION

Eugene F. Brigham
University of Florida

Louis C. Gapenski
University of Florida

Leo T. Gallant
St. Francis Xavier University

Holt, Rinehart and Winston of Canada, Limited

Toronto Montreal Chicago Ft. Worth
London Sydney Tokyo

The names of the corporations in this text are intended to be fictitious even though
the cases reflect situations that do occur in the world of business. Any similarity to
any existing corporation is purely coincidental.

Canadian Cataloguing in Publication Data
Brigham, Eugene F., 1930–
  Cases in financial management

1st Canadian ed.

ISBN 0-03-922795-2

1. Business enterprises — Finance — Case studies.
2. Corporations — Finance — Case studies.
I. Gapenski, Louis C. II. Gallant, Leo, 1948–
III. Title.

HG4026.B75 1991   658.15   C91-093147-X

Acquisitions Editor: Ron Fitzgerald
Developmental Editor: Andrew Livingston
Editorial Co-ordinator: Kerry Gibson
Production Editor: Sandra L. Meadow
Copy Editor: James Leahy
Cover Design: Dave Peters
Cover Photograph: Susan Dobson
Typesetting and Assembly: Bookman Typesetting Co.
Printing and Binding: Webcom Limited

⊗ This book was printed in Canada on acid-free paper.

1 2 3 4 5 96 95 94 93 92

Preface

Financial management can be a fascinating, exciting subject, yet students often regard it as being either too mechanical or too theoretical. However, one can overcome this misconception and demonstrate the inherent richness of the subject by relating the various topics to practices in the real world. If you illustrate a point by referring to an actual situation or case study, students' curiosity intensifies, their powers of concentration sharpen, and you are able to impart more knowledge than if you dealt strictly with abstractions or hypothetical situations.

To be most effective, the cases must (1) be related directly to the material covered in lectures, (2) contain a mix of numerical and conceptual questions, and (3) require no more than 3 to 5 hours of the students' time.

Relationship to Previous Casebooks

Cases in Managerial Finance was developed in the early 1970s, and new editions of that book were published by Brigham and various coauthors over the years, most recently by Brigham and Crum. The original set of cases was closely co-ordinated with the leading textbooks, but over the years the Crum-Brigham cases gradually lost their relationship with the texts. New theories, techniques, and empirical evidence were developed in the financial literature, and this material was worked into the textbooks but not into the cases. At the same time, the cases were becoming longer and more complex, and student preparation time increased. Finally, the old cases were not set up to effectively utilize computer spreadsheet programs such as *Lotus 1-2-3*, yet computerized analysis has become extremely important, indeed mandatory, if students are to be competitive in the marketplace.

In 1990 a new *Cases in Financial Management* by Brigham and Gapenski was released, primarily for the U.S. market. This new casebook drew to some extent from the old books, but most cases were new, and the carryovers were changed substantially. In effect, the authors went back to the original concept, and produced a set of cases that (1) address the major issues covered in the current mainline texts; (2) reinforce and illustrate the concepts, techniques, and theories covered in the texts; (3) contain both numerical questions and conceptual questions designed to stimulate discussion; (4) can typically be worked in 3 to 4 hours; and (5) serve to illustrate how computers can be used in financial analysis.

The Canadian Edition of *Cases in Financial Management* builds on the strength of the U.S. Edition but brings to the cases settings that are more familiar to Canadian students and incorporates some of the essential features of the Canadian tax, institutional, and economic environment.

Lotus 1-2-3 Models

As noted previously, *Lotus 1-2-3* and other computer spreadsheet programs have become extremely important in all aspects of finance, especially in financial management. Further, students are becoming increasingly computer literate, and more and more of them know at least the basics of *1-2-3* or a similar spreadsheet program when they come into the course. It is important that those students who have learned something about computers be given the opportunity to hone their skills, and this suggests that they be allowed (or required) to use spreadsheet programs to help analyze cases. If students have not learned anything about spreadsheets, it is perhaps even more important that they be exposed to them, because "functional literacy" in finance means at least some knowledge of spreadsheet analysis. These points make *Lotus 1-2-3*, which is by far the dominant spreadsheet package and is compatible with virtually all the other packages, an integral part of the cases.

However, there is a great deal of financial management material in a course, and to get through this material, you cannot get bogged down trying to teach students how to use computers. Also, in some schools students do not have ready access to PCs and the requisite software. Finally, some instructors are, unfortunately, not computer literate themselves, and thus they are reluctant to assign cases that require or even encourage computer analysis. Because of these factors, these cases are workable without using a computer. The analysis could, of course, all be done with a hand calculator, but the *1-2-3* models are far more efficient, especially if one asks "what if" questions. A frequently asked question is should you provide the models to the students, do you make students do all the *Lotus* programming themselves, or do you provide them with partially completed models? Most would conclude (1) that it would take students far too long to do all the modelling, (2) that if you gave them the completed model they would just use it as a black box to generate answers, so (3) that the only practical solution is to provide them with partially completed models. Therefore, the models provided to the students are the completed models with selected data and formula cells erased from them (with the data and formulas replaced with highlighted Xs). Two diskettes, one with the completed models and one with the partially completed models, are available to adopting instructors. Each instructor can, of course, delete even more from the models, or add back some formulas; what is optimal for one group of students may not be for another group.

Unfortunately, there is no such thing as an optimal partially completed model—the optimal amount to erase depends on what the instructor wants to accomplish and on the backgrounds of the students. If students are relatively proficient with *Lotus*, and if an instructor wants to emphasize financial modelling, then most of the cells should be erased, and the students should be required to develop the formulas for themselves. On the other hand, if the students do not have a very good background with *Lotus*, and if the instructor is more interested in having students see what the computer can do than in having them do the actual modelling, then only the minimum number of cells should be erased.

In the setup of the student models, fewer rather than more cells were erased, reflecting a preference to concentrate on financial issues as opposed to modelling. Also, students may have widely varying backgrounds—some are quite good with *Lotus*, while others know almost nothing about it. *Lotus*-oriented students can generally complete the student models in about a half hour (less for some models, slightly more for others), though they often get interested in the structure of the models and spend quite a bit of time going over them. The less-computer-oriented students have to spend more time, at least early in the term, but by the end of the semester, even they have learned enough about *Lotus* and the way our models are developed that they can complete them in about a half hour. Note that these times refer to the time necessary to complete the models and get them ready to run, not to the time spent actually using the models to do the required analysis. The analysis time can take from a half hour to two hours, depending on the nature of the case and the choices the student makes. Sometimes students get into elaborate sensitivity analyses and construct a number of tables and graphs (in addition to the ones provided—these graphs are generally macro-driven).

If an instructor wants to provide students with more or less complete models than those on the Student Diskette, he or she can delete from the completed models as many or as few cells as is desired, or just give the students the completed models.

The field of finance continues to undergo significant changes and advances. It is stimulating to participate in these developments, and it is hoped that these cases will help communicate the important issues in finance to future generations of students.

Acknowledgements

Cases in Financial Management reflects the contribution of many people. First and foremost, my thanks go to the U.S. authors Eugene Brigham and Louis Gapenski. I would also like to express my appreciation to the reviewers of this casebook, both Canadian and American, in particular Ben Amoaku-Adu (Wilfred Laurier University), Laurence Booth (University of Toronto) and Julia Scott (Bishop's University). Special thanks to my students at St. Francis Xavier University, my colleagues in the Department of Business Administration, especially John Sears, my secretary Anne Marie Durant and my research assistant Audrey MacAdam.

Finally, I would like to acknowledge the assistance and support of the staff at Holt, Rinehart and Winston of Canada especially Kerry Gibson, Andrew Livingston and Jim Leahy.

Leo Gallant
St. Francis Xavier University
Antigonish, Nova Scotia

Publisher's Note to Instructors and Students

This casebook is a key component of your course. If you are the instructor of this course, you undoubtedly considered a number of casebooks carefully before choosing this as the one that would work best for your students and you. The authors and publishers of this book spent considerable time and money to ensure its high quality, and we appreciate your recognition of this effort and accomplishment.

If you are a student we are confident that this casebook will help you to meet the objectives of your course. You will also find it helpful after the course is finished as a valuable addition to your personal library.

As well, please do not forget that photocopying copyright work means the authors lose royalties that are rightfully theirs. This loss will discourage them from writing another edition of this text or other books; doing so would simply not be worth their time and effort. If this happens we all lose—students, instructors, authors, and publishers.

Since we want to hear what you think about this book, please be sure to send us the stamped reply card at the end of the text. This will help us to continue publishing high-quality books for your course.

Contents

I

Fundamental Concepts 1

1

Risk and Return – Wellington Securities, Inc. (A) 2

2

Bond and Stock Valuation – Wellington Securities, Inc. (B) 8

II

Cost of Capital 13

3

Cost of Capital – Upland Technologies, Inc. 14

4

Divisional Hurdle Rates – Claremont Manufacturing Company 19

III

Capital Structure 27

5

Financial Leverage – Floral Designs, Inc. 28

6

Capital Structure Policy – Canola Copiers, Incorporated 35

IV

Capital Budgeting 41

7

Capital Budgeting Decision Methods – Clarke Controls 42

8

Cash Flow Estimation – McReath Corporation (A) 47

9

Risk Analysis in Capital Budgeting – McReath Corporation (B) 53

10
Capital Budgeting with Staged Entry – Computer-ese Incorporated *60*

V
Dividend Policy 67

11
Dividend Policy – Northern Paper Company *68*

VI
Long-Term Financing Decisions 75

12
Going Public – Capital City Savings and Loan *76*

13
Bond Refunding – East Coast Electric *81*

14
Lease Analysis – Bunbury Chemical Company *87*

15
Financing with Convertibles and Warrants – Weaver Foods, Inc. *94*

VII
Working Capital Management 103

16
Working Capital Policy and Financing – Kelsey Furniture Company *104*

17
Inventory Management – LakeSide Marine Corporation *111*

18
Cash Budgeting – MacAdam Enterprises *117*

19
Credit Policy – Kiddyland Clothes, Inc. *127*

VIII
Financial Analysis and Forecasting 133

20
Financial Analysis and Forecasting – National Trailer Company (A) *134*

21
Financial Forecasting – Real Estate Management Systems Company   *145*

IX
Bankruptcy and Mergers   153

22
Bankruptcy and Reorganization – National Trailer Company (B)   *154*

23
Merger Analysis – Handyware, Inc.   *158*

I

Fundamental Concepts

Case 1
Risk and Return Wellington Securities, Inc. (A)

Case 2
Bond and Stock Valuation Wellington Securities, Inc. (B)

1

Risk and Return

Wellington Securities, Inc. (A)

Wellington Securities is a regional brokerage house based in Calgary. Although the firm is only 20 years old, it has prospered by following a simple goal—providing personal brokerage services to small investors. Charles Mitchell, the firm's founder and president, is satisfied with Wellington's progress, yet he is apprehensive about the future, as more and more of the firm's customers are buying mutual funds rather than individual stocks and bonds. Thus, even though the number of customers per office has been increasing because of population growth, the number of transactions per customer has been decreasing, and hence sales growth has slackened.

Mitchell believes that this trend will continue, so he has been actively expanding his product line in an effort to increase sales volume. As a first step, Wellington began offering trust and portfolio management services 5 years ago. Many of the trust clients are retirees who are interested primarily in current income rather than capital gains. Thus, an average portfolio consists mostly of bonds and high-yield stocks. The stock component is heavily weighted with electric utilities, an industry that has traditionally paid high dividends. For example, the average electric company's dividend yield was about 8 percent at the beginning of 1988 versus an average stock's yield of 3.5 percent.

Until recently, Wellington had no in-house security analysts—all stock and bond selections were based on research provided by subscription services. However, these services were becoming increasingly costly, and the volume of portfolio management was reaching the point where an in-house analyst was cost-justified. Because most of its portfolios were heavily weighted with electric utilities, Wellington created its first analyst position to track this industry, and Mitchell hired Louise Richards, a recent graduate of the University of Alberta, to fill the job.

Richards reported to work in early January 1990, jubilant at having the opportunity to put to use the skills she had worked so hard to learn. Mitchell then informed her that her first task would be to conduct a seminar for a group of Wellington customers on stock investments, including the effects of different securities on portfolio performance. Richards was asked to pick an electric utility, assess its riskiness, develop an estimate of its required rate of return on equity, and then explain all this to a group of Wellington's customers.

Richards's first step—choosing the company—was simple. She had been born and raised in Red Deer, so she picked Prairie Utilities Limited. Prairie Utilities is engaged in electrical power generation and distribution throughout Alberta, as well as natural gas production and distribution. Next, she set about finding some information on the company. Richards remembered using the *Financial Post Corporate Data Base* during her student days, so she turned to this source first. Then she spent a few days reviewing industry trends to gain a historical perspective.

Electric utilities are granted monopolies to provide electric service in a given geographical area. In exchange for the franchise, the company is subjected to regulation over both the prices it may charge and the quality of its service. In theory, regulation acts to prevent the company from abusing its monopoly position, and its prices are set to mimic the prices that would occur if the firm were operating under perfect competition. Under such competition, the firm would earn its cost of capital, no more and no less.

Back in the 1950s and much of the 1960s, electric utilities were in an ideal position. Their costs were declining because of technological advances and economies of scale in generation and distribution, and this made everyone happy—managers, regulators, stockholders, and customers. However, the situation changed dramatically during the 1970s, when inflation, along with high gas and oil prices, pushed construction and operating costs to levels that were unimaginable just a few years earlier. The result was a massive change in the economics of the industry and in how investors viewed electric utilities.

Today the industry is facing many challenges; among them are (1) cogeneration, (2) diversification, (3) deregulation, and (4) nuclear generation. Cogeneration is the combined production of electricity and thermal power, usually steam. Most electric companies use coal or nuclear energy to generate electricity. In the 1980s, though, oil and gas prices dropped sharply, making them cheaper fuel sources for generating electricity. However, one cannot burn gas or oil in a coal or nuclear plant. The changed fuel-cost situation, combined with the need for steam, made it profitable for many industrial customers to switch to cogeneration. This, in turn, has made it very difficult for utilities to forecast industrial demand. Also, since utilities must buy any surplus power generated by their former customers, the companies with cogeneration plants are, in effect, competing with the electric companies.

At the same time, many electric utilities now have cash flows that exceed their immediate needs. Most companies finished major plant construction programs in the early 1980s, and they are now reaping large depreciation flows. Some in the industry believe that utilities should use these cash flows to diversify into nonregulated industries. The rationale is that diversification smooths out the financial risks of the regulated business and affords companies an opportunity to earn returns above those allowed by regulation. To facilitate diversification, many electric utilities, including Prairie Utilities Ltd., have formed both regulated and nonregulated subsidiaries. Diversification, however, does have a potential downside for both utility customers (ratepayers) and stockholders. Ratepayers are supposed to pay the costs associated with producing and delivering power, plus enough to cover the utility's cost of capital. However, a diversified utility could, theoretically, allocate some corporate costs that should be assigned to the unregulated (diversified) subsidiaries to the regulated utility. This would cause the reported profits to be abnormally high for the unregulated business and, in effect, ratepayers would be subsidizing the nonregulated businesses. The corporation's overall rate of return would be excessive, because it would be earning the regulated cost of capital on utility operations and more than a competitive return on unregulated operations. Of course, regulators are aware of all this, so their auditors are always on the alert to detect and prevent improper cost allocations.

There are two significant risks to stockholders from utility diversification. First, there is the chance that utility executives, who generally have limited exposure to intense competition, will fail in the competitive unregulated markets they enter. In that case, money that could have been paid out as dividends will have been lost in business ventures that turned out to be unprofitable. Second, if the diversified activities are highly profitable, causing the overall corporation to earn a high rate of return, then regulators might reduce the returns allowed on the utility operations. There is always a question as to what a company's cost of capital really is, and hence what rate of return the utility commission should allow it to earn. Therefore, it is easier for a commission to set the allowed rate of return at the low end of any reasonable range if the company is highly profitable because of successful unregulated businesses. Thus, it has been argued that diversified utilities might be getting into a "no-win" situation, and, as one analyst put it, its stockholders are in a "heads you win, tails I lose" situation.

There is also much discussion at present about the deregulation of the electricity markets per se, and there is much controversy over the forced use of "wheeling," whereby a customer (usually a large industrial customer) buys power from some other party but gets delivery over the transmission lines of the utility in whose service area it operates. This situation has occurred to a large extent in the gas industry, where large customers have contracted directly with producers and then forced (through legal actions) pipeline companies to deliver the gas.

Another problem facing many, but not all, electric companies relates to nuclear plants. A few decades ago, nuclear power was thought by many to be the wave of the future in electric generation. It was widely believed that

Table 1
Estimated Return Distributions

State of the Economy	Probability	Estimated Total Return			
		1-year Government of Canada Bond	Prairie Utilities Ltd.	Goldbrook	TSE 300 Fund
Recession	0.10	8.0%	−8.0%	18.0%	−15.0%
Below average	0.20	8.0	2.0	23.0	0.0
Average	0.40	8.0	14.0	7.0	15.0
Above average	0.20	8.0	25.0	−3.0	30.0
Boom	0.10	8.0	33.0	2.0	45.0

nuclear power was cleaner and cheaper than coal, oil, and gas generation. However, the 1979 accident at Three Mile Island almost instantly reversed the future of nuclear power. Plans for many plants under construction at that time were cancelled, while the costs of completing the remaining plants skyrocketed, and many partially completed plants had to be retrofitted with new safety devices. As a result, the cost of power from new nuclear plants rose dramatically. Further, several provinces have considered closing nuclear plants. No closures have taken place so far, but another accident could lead to the closing of many operating plants, at a great cost to investors.

With this industry overview in mind, Louise Richards developed the data in Table 1 on returns expected in the coming year. Prairie Utilities is the stock of primary interest; Goldbrook Explorations, Inc., is a domestic gold mining company; and the TSE 300 Fund is a mutual fund that invests in the stocks that make up the TSE 300 average. Richards's final preparatory step was to outline some questions that she believed to be relevant to the task at hand. See if you can answer the questions she developed.

Questions

1. Why is the Government of Canada bond return in Table 1 shown to be independent of the state of the economy? Is the return on a 1-year Government of Canada bond risk free?

2. Calculate the expected rate of return on each of the four alternatives listed in Table 1. Based solely on expected returns, which of the potential investments appears best?

3. Now calculate the standard deviations and coefficients of variation of returns for the four alternatives. What type of risk do these statistics measure? Is the standard deviation or the coefficient of variation the better measure? How do the alternatives compare when risk is consid-

ered? (Hint: For the TSE 300, the standard deviation = 16.4%; for Goldbrook Explorations, the standard deviation = 9.1%.)

4. Suppose an investor forms a stock portfolio by investing $10 000 in Goldbrook Explorations and $10 000 in Prairie Utilities.
   a. What would be the portfolio's expected rate of return, standard deviation, and coefficient of variation? How does this compare with values for the individual stocks? What characteristic of the two investments makes risk reduction possible?
   b. What do you think would happen to the portfolio's expected rate of return and standard deviation if the portfolio contained 75 percent Goldbrook? If it contained 75 percent Prairie Utilities? If you are using the *Lotus* model for this case, calculate the expected returns and standard deviations for a portfolio mix of 0 percent Prairie Utilities, 10 percent Prairie Utilities, 20 percent Prairie Utilities, and so on, up to 100 percent Prairie Utilities.

5. Now consider a portfolio consisting of $10 000 in Prairie Utilities and $10 000 in the TSE 300 Fund. Would this portfolio have the same risk-reducing effect as the Goldbrook–Prairie Utilities portfolio considered in Question 4? Explain. If you are using the *Lotus* model, construct a portfolio using Prairie Utilities and the TSE 300. What are the expected returns and standard deviations for a portfolio mix of 0 percent Prairie Utilities, 10 percent Prairie Utilities, 20 percent Prairie Utilities, and so on, up to 100 percent Prairie Utilities?

6. Suppose an investor starts with a portfolio consisting of one randomly selected stock.
   a. What would happen to the portfolio's risk if more and more randomly selected stocks were added?
   b. What are the implications for investors? Do portfolio effects impact the way investors should think about the riskiness of individual securities? Would you expect this to affect companies' costs of capital?
   c. Explain the differences between total risk, diversifiable (company-specific) risk, and market risk.
   d. Assume that you choose to hold a single-stock portfolio. Should you expect to be compensated for all of the risk that you bear?

7. Now change Table 1 by crossing out the state of the economy and probability columns, and replacing them with Year 1, Year 2, Year 3, Year 4, and Year 5. (In effect, you are changing the data from expectational to historical.) Then, plot three lines on a scatter diagram showing the returns on the TSE 300 Fund (the market) on the x axis and (1) Government of Canada bond returns, (2) Prairie Utilities returns, and (3) Goldbrook Explorations returns on the y axis. What are these lines called? Estimate the slope coefficient of each line. What is the slope

coefficient called, and what is its significance? What is the significance of the distance between the plot points and the regression line? (Note: If you have a calculator with statistical functions or if you are using the *Lotus* model, use linear regression to find the slope coefficients.)

8. Plot the Security Market Line. (Hint: Use Table 1 data to obtain the risk-free rate and the required rate of return on the market.) What is the required rate of return on Prairie Utilities' stock using a beta estimate of 0.6? Based on the CAPM analysis, should investors buy Prairie Utilities' stock?

9. What would happen to Prairie Utilities' required rate of return if inflation expectations increased by 3 percentage points above the estimate embedded in the 8.0 percent risk-free rate? Now go back to the original inflation estimate, where $k_{RF} = 8\%$, and indicate what would happen to Prairie Utilities' required rate of return if investors' risk aversion increased so that the market risk premium rose from 7 percent to 8 percent. Now go back to the original conditions ($k_{RF} = 8\%$, $RP_M = 7\%$) and assume that Prairie Utilities' beta rose from 0.6 to 1.0. What effect would this have on the required rate of return?

10. What is the efficient markets hypothesis (EMH)? What impact does this theory have on decisions concerning the investment in securities? Is it applicable to real assets such as plant and equipment? What impact does the EMH have on corporate financing decisions? Should Charles Mitchell be concerned about the EMH when he considers adding to his staff of security analysts? Explain.
    (The following questions require an introductory knowledge of business risk and financial risk. They may be assigned as part of the case or may be discussed in class.)

11. Assume that non-utility businesses will account for much of Prairie Utilities' earnings growth. Does this fact affect the validity of the 0.6 beta for decision purposes? If so, how? (Hint: Beta estimates were based on historical returns over the past 5 years.)

12. Prairie Utilities' long-term debt ratio (Long-term debt/Total assets) has declined from 51.1 percent in 1982 to an estimated 41.5 percent in 1990 and is projected to be 37.5 percent for the 1992–1994 period. What impact does this have on Prairie Utilities' riskiness, and hence on its beta and its required rate of return on equity?

2

Bond and Stock Valuation

Wellington Securities, Inc. (B)[*]

Louise Richards, the recently hired utility analyst for Wellington Securities, completed her first assignment with flying colours (Wellington Securities, Inc. [A]). After she presented her seminar on risk and return, many customers were clamouring for a second lecture. Therefore, Charles Mitchell, Wellington's president, gave Richards her second task: determine the value of Prairie Utilities' bonds, common stock, and preferred stock, and prepare a seminar to explain the valuation process to the firm's customers.

Richards examined Prairie Utilities' latest annual report, especially note 7 to the consolidated financial statements. This note lists Prairie Utilities' long-term debt obligations, including its first mortgage bonds, instalment contracts, and term loans. Table 1 contains information on three of the first mortgage bonds listed in the annual report.

A concern that immediately occurred to Richards was the phenomenon of "event risk." Recently, many investors have shied away from the industrial bond market because of the current wave of leveraged buyouts (LBOs) and debt-financed corporate takeovers. These takeovers are financed by the issuing of large amounts of new debt—often high-risk "junk" bonds—which causes the credit rating of the target firm's existing bonds to drop, the required rate of return to increase, and the price of the bonds to decline.

Richards wondered if this trend would affect the required returns on Prairie Utilities' outstanding bonds. Upon reflection, she concluded that Prairie Utilities' bonds would be much less vulnerable to such event risk because Prairie Utilities is a regulated public utility. Public utilities and banks are less vulnerable to takeovers and leveraged buyouts, primarily because their regulators would have to approve such restructurings, and it is unlikely

---

*It is not necessary to have worked Part A of the case to work Part B.

Table 1
Partial Long-Term Debt Listing for Prairie Utilities

Face Amount	Coupon Rate	Maturity Year	Year to Maturity
$ 48 000 000	4½%	1994	5
32 000 000	8¼	2004	15
100 000 000	12⅝	2114	25

Note : To simplify the case, the terms stated here are modified slightly from the actual terms.

that they would permit the level of debt needed for an LBO. Therefore, many investors have turned to government bonds, mortgage-backed issues, and utility bonds in lieu of publicly traded corporate bonds. As a result, Richards concluded that the effect, if any, of the increased concern about event risk would be to *lower* Prairie Utilities' cost of bond financing.

With these considerations in mind, your task is to help Richards pass her second hurdle at Wellington Securities by helping her answer the following questions.

Questions

Preliminary note: Some of our answers were generated using a computer model that carried things out 15 decimal places. Therefore, you can expect small rounding differences if your answers are obtained using a financial calculator. These differences are not material.

1. To begin, assume that it is now January 1, 1990, and that each bond in Table 1 matures on December 31 of the year listed. Further, assume that each bond has a $1000 par value, each had a 30-year maturity when it was issued, and each bond currently has a 10 percent required nominal rate of return.
   a. Why do the bonds' coupon rates vary so widely?
   b. What would be the value of each bond if they had annual coupon payments?
   c. Prairie Utilities' bonds, like virtually all bonds, actually pay interest semiannually. What is each bond's value under these conditions? Is each bond currently selling at a discount or at a premium?
   d. What is the effective annual rate of return implied by the values obtained in Part c?
   e. Would you expect a semiannual-payment bond to sell at a higher or lower price than an otherwise equivalent annual-payment bond? Now look at the 5-year bond in Parts b and c; are the prices shown consistent with your expectations? Explain.

2. Now, regardless of your answers to Question 1, assume that the 5-year bond is selling for $800.00, the 15-year bond is selling for $865.49, and the 25-year bond is selling for $1220.00. (Use these prices, and assume semiannual coupons, for the remainder of the questions.)
   a. Explain the meaning of the term "yield to maturity."
   b. What is the nominal (as opposed to effective annual) yield to maturity (YTM) on each bond?
   c. What is the effective annual YTM on each issue?
   d. In comparing bond yields with the yields on other securities, should the nominal or effective YTM be used? Explain.

3. Suppose Prairie Utilities has a second bond with 25 years left to maturity (in addition to the one listed in Table 1), which has a coupon rate of $7\frac{3}{8}$ percent and a market price of $747.48.
   a. What is (1) the nominal and (2) the effective annual YTM on this bond?
   b. What is the current yield on each of the 25-year bonds?
   c. What is each bond's expected price on January 1, 1991, and its capital gains yield for 1990, assuming no change in interest rates? (Hint: Remember that the nominal required rate of return on each bond is 10.18 percent.)
   d. What would happen to the prices of each bond over time? (Again, assume constant future interest rates.)
   e. What is the expected total (percentage) return on each bond during 1990?
   f. If you were a tax-paying investor, which bond would you prefer? Why? What impact would this preference have on the prices, and hence YTMs, of the two bonds?

4. Consider the riskiness of the bonds.
   a. Explain the difference between interest rate risk and reinvestment rate risk.
   b. Which of the bonds listed in Table 1 has the most interest rate risk? Why?
   c. Assume that you bought 5-year, 15-year, and 25-year bonds, all with a 10 percent coupon rate and semiannual coupons, at their $1000 par values. Which bond's value would be affected most if interest rates rose to 13 percent? Which would be affected least? If you are using the *Lotus* model, calculate the new value of each bond.
   d. Assume that your investment horizon (or expected holding period) is 25 years. Which of the bonds listed in Table 1 has the greatest reinvestment rate risk? Why? What is a type of bond you could buy to eliminate reinvestment rate risk?
   e. Assume that you plan to keep your money invested, and to reinvest all interest receipts, for 5 years. Assume also that you bought the

5-year bond in Table 1 for $800, and interest rates suddenly fell to 5.0 percent and remained at that level for 5 years. Set up a time line that could be used to calculate the actual realized rate of return on the bond, but do not (necessarily) complete the calculations. (Hint: Note that each interest receipt must be compounded to the terminal date and summed, along with the maturity value. Then, the rate of return that equates this terminal value to the initial value of the bond is the bond's realized return.) Assume that the answer is 9.16%. How does that value compare with your expected rate of return? What would have happened if interest rates had risen to 15% rather than fallen to 5%? How would the results have differed if you had bought the 25-year bond rather than the 5-year bond? Do these results suggest that you would be better or worse off if you bought bonds and then rates changed? Explain.

f. Today, many bond market participants are speculators as opposed to long-term investors. If you thought interest rates were going to fall from current levels, what type of bond would you buy to maximize short-term capital gains?

5. Now assume that the 15-year bond is callable after 5 years at $1050.
   a. What is its yield to call (YTC) assuming that it is selling for $865.49?
   b. Do you think it is likely that the bond will be called?

6. Prairie Utilities has $84 956 000 of preferred stock outstanding.
   a. Suppose its Series A, which has a $100 par value and pays a 4.32 percent cumulative dividend, currently sells for $48.00 per share. What is its nominal expected rate of return? Its effective annual rate of return? (Hint: Remember that dividends are paid quarterly. Also, assume that this issue is perpetual.)
   b. Suppose Series F, with a $100 par value and a 9.75 percent cumulative dividend, has a mandatory sinking fund provision. Of the 300 000 total shares outstanding, 60 000 must be redeemed annually at par beginning on December 31, 1990. If the nominal required rate of return is 8.0 percent, what is the current (January 1, 1990) value per share?

7. Now consider Prairie Utilities' common stock. Estimates of Prairie Utilities' 5-year dividend growth rate average 6.0 percent. Assume that Prairie Utilities' stock traded on January 1, 1989 for $22.25. Assume for now that the 6.0 percent growth rate is expected to continue indefinitely.
   a. What was Prairie Utilities' expected rate of return at the beginning of 1989? (Hint: D_1 is estimated to be $1.40 at the start of 1989.)
   b. What was the expected dividend yield and expected capital gains yield on January 1, 1989?
   c. What is the relationship between dividend yield and capital gains yield over time under constant-growth assumptions?

    d. What conditions must hold to use the constant-growth (Gordon) model? Do many "real world" stocks satisfy the constant-growth assumptions?

8. Suppose you believe that Prairie Utilities' 6.0 percent dividend growth rate will only hold for 5 years. After that, the growth rate will return to Prairie Utilities' historical 10-year average of 8.5 percent.

    a. What was the value of Prairie Utilities' stock on January 1, 1989, if the required rate of return is 13.5 percent?

    b. What is the expected stock price at the end of 1989 assuming that the stock is in equilibrium?

    c. What is the expected dividend yield, capital gains yield, and total return for 1989?

    d. Suppose Prairie Utilities' dividend was expected to remain constant at $1.40 for the next 5 years, and then grow at a constant 6 percent rate. If the required rate of return is 13.5 percent, would Prairie Utilities' stock value be higher or lower than your answer to Part a? If you are using the *Lotus* model for this case, calculate the dividend yield, capital gains yield, and total yield from 1989 through 1993.

    e. Prairie Utilities' stock price was $22.25 at the beginning of 1989. Using the growth rates given in the introduction to this question, what is the stock's expected rate of return?

9. Common stocks are usually valued assuming annual dividends, even though dividends are actually paid quarterly. This is because the dividend stream is so uncertain that the use of a quarterly model is not warranted. The quarterly constant growth valuation model is

$$\hat{P}_0 = \frac{D_{q1}(1+k)^{0.75} + D_{q2}(1+k)^{0.05} + D_{q3}(1+k)^{0.25} + D_{q4}(1+k)^0}{k-g}$$

where $\hat{P}_0$ is the stock's value and D_{q1} is the dividend in Quarter 1. Note that this model assumes that dividend growth occurs once each year rather than at every quarter. Assume that Prairie Utilities' next four quarterly dividends are $1.40/4 = $0.35 each; that k, the annual required rate of return, is 12.5 percent, and that g is a constant 6.0 percent. What is Prairie Utilities' value according to the quarterly model?

II

Cost of Capital

Case 3
Cost of Capital Upland Technologies, Inc.

Case 4
Divisional Hurdle Rates Claremont Manufacturing Company

3

Cost of Capital

Upland Technologies, Inc.

Upland Technologies was founded 10 years ago by a group of scientists and engineers in the Ottawa area. The firm's goal was to attain a leadership position in the electronic image recording market. Electronic imaging is a specialized technology that fills an important need for major firms marketing medical diagnostic imaging systems. By concentrating technology and production resources, Upland was able to produce a superior film recorder at a price below its competitors' development and manufacturing costs. Upland quickly became the leader in the video photography market, providing original equipment manufacturers (OEMs) such as GE, Philips, Toshiba, and Siemens with the hardcopy film recording devices used in their magnetic resonance and CAT scanners.

Over the years, Upland noted that some aspect of electronic imaging will eventually be used by almost all businesses that use computers. As the need develops to input image data to a computer, or to output image data to hardcopy, potential applications of Upland's technologies are created. Recognizing this, Upland's management is positioning the firm both for broader participation in medical diagnostic imaging and for new applications in computer graphics and industrial imaging.

At present, Upland has two divisions: (1) Medical Applications and (2) Industrial Applications. The goal of the Medical Applications Division is to expand the number and use of Upland's products in market areas where the firm currently has a presence. The division's most recent product is a laser-based imaging system that will support the totally digital radiography systems of the future. With this system, radiologists are no longer constrained by the limitations of direct X-ray exposure on film. Rather, computers now process digitized electronic X-ray images, amplify diagnostic information, and display the result on a CRT. When the most useful "picture" is obtained, Upland's imaging system is used to create the hardcopy.

Table 1
Upland Technologies: Balance Sheet
for the Year Ended December 31, 1990
(Millions of Dollars)

Cash	$ 5.1	Accounts payable	$ 3.8
Accounts receivable	$ 26.4	Accruals	$ 5.0
Inventory	$ 56.1	Notes payable	$ 1.3
Current assets	$ 87.6	Current liabilities	$ 10.1
Net fixed assets	$ 26.3	Long-term debt	$ 40.8
		Preferred stock	$ 9.7
		Common stock	$ 53.3
Total assets	$113.9	Total claims	$113.9

The newer Industrial Applications Division's goal is to become a market force in the rapidly developing areas of computer graphics and industrial imaging. The basic technology used here has many similarities to that used in medical imaging, and hence Upland's managers predict a rosy future for this division. Two products are already being sold: a personal colour recorder and a thermal transfer colour printer. Intended for use with the IBM PC line, these products make fast, high-quality, in-house graphics a reality.

Thus far, Upland's growth has been somewhat helter-skelter, with superior technological know-how easily overcoming any deficiencies in managerial decision making. Now, as competition stiffens and the firm moves into uncharted waters, Upland's board of directors is keenly aware that the firm must apply state-of-the-art techniques to its managerial decisions as well as to its product lines. As a first priority, the board has directed Upland's CEO, Steve Milne, to develop an estimate for the firm's cost of capital, which the board plans to use at its next meeting, which will focus on new product decisions. Milne, in turn, directed Upland's financial manager, Pat Murphy, to have a cost of capital estimate on his desk in one week.

To begin, Pat reviewed Upland's 1990 balance sheet, which is contained in Table 1. Next, Pat assembled the following relevant data:

(1) The firm's tax rate is 40 percent.

(2) Upland's 12 percent semiannual coupon bonds with 15 years remaining to maturity are not actively traded. However, a block did trade last week at a price of $1153.72 per bond.

(3) Upland uses short-term debt only to fund cyclical working capital needs.

(4) The firm's 10 percent, $100 par value, quarterly dividend perpetual preferred stock is traded on the Toronto Stock Exchange (TSE). Its current price is $113.10 per share; however, Upland would incur flotation costs of $2.00 per share on a new issue.

(5) Upland's common stock is currently selling on the TSE at $50 per share. The firm's last dividend (D_0) was $1.73, and dividends are expected to grow at roughly a 10 percent annual rate in the foreseeable future.

(6) The firm's historical beta, as measured by a stock analyst who follows the firm, is 1.2. The current yield on long-term (20-year) Government of Canada bonds is 7.0 percent, and a prominent investment securities firm has recently estimated the market risk premium to be 6.0 percentage points.

(7) The required rate of return on an average (A-rated) company's long-term debt is 9.0 percent.

(8) Upland's investment dealer believes that a new common stock issue would require flotation costs, including market pressure and negative signalling, of 30.0 percent.

(9) The firm's market value target capital structure is 30 percent debt, 10 percent preferred stock, and 60 percent common stock.

(10) The firm is forecasting retained earnings of $1 200 000 and a depreciation expense of $3 000 000 for the coming year.

With these data at hand, consider the following questions that Pat must address in his analysis.

Questions

1. What sources of capital should be included in Upland's cost-of-capital estimate? Should the component cost estimates be before-tax or after-tax? Should they be historical (embedded) or new (marginal)?

2. Consider Upland's cost of debt.
   a. What is the cost estimate for this component?
   b. Should flotation costs be included? Explain.
   c. Should the nominal cost of debt or the effective rate be used? Explain.
   d. How valid is the estimate based on 15-year bonds if Upland typically issues 30-year long-term debt?
   e. Suppose Upland's outstanding debt had not been recently traded. What other methods could be used to estimate the firm's debt cost?
   f. Would it matter if the bonds currently outstanding were callable? Explain.

3. Now consider the firm's cost of preferred stock.
   a. What is the preferred cost estimate?
   b. Upland's preferred stock is more risky to investors than its debt, yet its before-tax yield to investors is lower than the yield on Upland's

debt. Does this suggest that you have made a mistake in your calculations?

   c. Now suppose that Upland's preferred had a mandatory redemption provision that specified that the firm must redeem the issue in 5 years at a price of $110 per share. What would Upland's cost of preferred have been in this situation?

4. Now consider the cost of common equity.
   a. Why is there a cost associated with retained earnings?
   b. What is Upland's estimated cost of retained earnings using the CAPM approach?
   c. Is the long-term Government of Canada bond rate a better estimate of the risk-free rate than the T-bill rate?
   d. How do historical betas, adjusted historical betas, and fundamental betas differ? Do you think Upland's historical beta is a good measure of its future market risk? Explain.
   e. How can the market risk premium be estimated?

5. a. What is the discounted cash flow (DCF) cost of retained earnings estimate?
   b. Suppose that Upland, over the last few years, has averaged 15 percent return on equity (ROE) and paid out about 20 percent of net income as dividends. Can this information be used to help estimate the firm's future growth rate, g?

6. What is the bond-yield-plus-risk-premium estimate for Upland's cost of retained earnings?

7. What is your final estimate for k_s? Explain how you weighted the estimates of the three methods.

8. What is the estimate for Upland's cost of new common stock, k_e?

9. a. Construct Upland's marginal cost of capital (MCC) schedule. At what amount of new investment would Upland be forced to issue new common stock? (Ignore depreciation at this point.)
   b. Would Upland's MCC schedule remain constant beyond the retained earnings break point regardless of the amount of new capital required? (Again, ignore depreciation.)

10. What impact does depreciation have on Upland's MCC schedule? Would the inclusion of depreciation affect the acceptability of proposed capital projects?

11. Could the corporate cost of capital developed in Question 9 be used at the divisional level? That is, is a single cost of capital appropriate for both the Medical Applications Division and the Industrial Applications Division? If not, what type of adjustment should be made?

12. What are Upland's book value weights of debt, preferred stock, and common stock? (Hint: Consider only long-term sources of capital.) Should book value or market value weights be used in estimating a firm's overall cost of capital?

4

Divisional Hurdle
Rates

Claremont Manufacturing Company

Claremont Manufacturing Company is a multidivisional producer of (1) abrasive products, especially high-quality electric sanders and sandpaper for home use; (2) industrial grinders and sharpeners; and (3) coated ceramics used in the aerospace and other industries where surface bonding agents with high strength and resistance to high temperatures are required. The company also has a division that is active in real estate development; the division was started several years ago, when a large tract of land just west of Surrey, British Columbia, which Claremont had acquired for its mineral potential many years ago, became valuable for real estate development. Because of the nature of the various product lines, the company was divided into four separate divisions in 1980: the Home Products Division, the Equipment Manufacturing Division, the Ceramic Coatings Division, and the Real Estate Division. This arrangement has worked reasonably well, but frictions have developed among the divisions, and Claremont's stock has not performed as well as others in the industry.

A special committee was appointed by the board of directors, and all senior executives, including Phillip Calhoun, the firm's financial vice-president, have been asked to identify problems and then to recommend ways to eliminate them. Calhoun found numerous small ways in which financial operations could be changed for the better, but only one area presented a major problem—the financial planning process and, specifically, the way risk is taken into consideration in this process. Currently, Claremont does not formally incorporate differential risk into project evaluations, and the capital budgeting process works like this:

(1)   A corporate hurdle rate is developed by the corporate treasurer.

(2)   Projected cash inflows and outflows are estimated for each potential project by each division, and these project data are entered into the

computerized capital budgeting system, which then calculates each project's NPV, IRR, MIRR, and payback period.

(3)   If a project's NPV is positive and large, if its IRR and MIRR are at least 3 percentage points above the corporate hurdle rate, and if its payback period is 4 years or less, then the project will usually be accepted. On the other hand, if the NPV is negative, if the IRR and MIRR are well below the corporate hurdle rate, and if the payback period is long (8 years or more), the project will almost always be rejected. Projects with NPVs close to zero, IRRs and MIRRs[1] close to the corporate hurdle rate, and paybacks in the 5- to 7-year range are considered marginal, and these projects are accepted or rejected depending on management's confidence in the cash flow forecasts; on the project's long-run, strategic effects on the firm; and on the availability of capital.

Although everyone agrees that an average project in the Ceramic Coatings Division is substantially riskier than an average project in the Home Products Division, no explicit allowance is made for this differential risk. As a result of this procedure, substantially more capital has been invested in the Ceramic Coatings Division, and in riskier projects from all divisions, than otherwise would have been allotted, because high-risk projects typically offer high returns. Calhoun recognizes that such problems are inherent in an informal risk adjustment process. Also, his assistant, Jean Lam, recently concluded her annual review of the company's budgeting process with two strong recommendations: (1) that project risk be given more formal consideration in the capital budgeting process, and (2) that the idea of different hurdle rates for different divisions be investigated. Calhoun appreciates the need for some sort of formal risk evaluation system, but he is afraid that top management will resist such an approach unless he can demonstrate why so radical a departure from past practices is necessary, and also show how not using such procedures has hurt the company in the past. The job of proving the need for, and then designing a risk evaluation system will not be easy—it will require the co-operation of many managers from all parts of the organization.

With the annual budget completed and no urgent problems facing him, Calhoun set up a team to study the question of risk-adjusted hurdle rates. Helen Findley, the corporate treasurer; Ken Godfrey, the corporate capital budgeting director; and the four divisional controllers comprised the study group. Jean Lam was assigned to the study group and, at the end of its first meeting, was asked to research the following questions, plus any others she regarded as important:

---

1   The MIRR is found in three steps: (1) compound all net operating cash inflows forward to the terminal year at the cost of capital; (2) sum the compounded cash inflows to obtain the *terminal value* of the inflows; and (3) find the discount rate that forces the present value of the terminal value to equal the PV of the net investment outlays. This discount rate is defined as the MIRR.

(1) Should hurdle rates be established for each division, for each product line within a division, or on an individual project basis?

(2) How should project risk be measured?

(3) How should capital structure, or debt capacity, be handled? This issue is important because the Real Estate Division's manager, Hugh Edwards, has been complaining that he needs to use more debt if he is to compete effectively with other firms in the real estate development business.

Lam decided that a reasonable place to start her inquiry was to focus on the concept of market risk, which she had studied as a student. After several discussions, she found that Claremont's senior management agreed that the firm's risk, as seen by well-diversified investors, is the key determinant of its cost of equity capital. The senior managers also agreed that investors estimate risk, in large part although not exclusively, by a stock's relative volatility to the market as measured by its beta coefficient. Lam had earlier conducted a study of the determinants of Claremont's beta, and concluded that the corporate beta is a weighted average of the betas that the four divisions would have if they were operated as separate firms. Lam then set up the following table:

Division	Proportion of Corporate Assets (1)	Estimated Divisional Beta (2)	Product $(1) \times (2)$ = (3)
Real Estate	0.05	0.60	0.030
Ceramic Coatings	0.10	1.95	0.195
Equipment Manufacturing	0.30	1.05	0.315
Home Products	0.55	0.65	0.358
	1.00		

Weighted average corporate beta = $\underline{0.898} \approx \underline{0.90}$

In estimating the divisional betas, Lam (1) examined the betas for publicly held real estate, abrasives, general manufacturing, and special coatings companies, and (2) looked at the volatility of earnings in each division vis-à-vis earnings on the TSE 300 Index. The betas as estimated by both of these methods, for each division, were then averaged, and this average was used as the divisional beta reported in the tabulation. The weighted average of the divisional betas, 0.9, is quite close to Claremont's beta coefficient as reported by leading brokerage dealers.

Lam then used these divisional betas to set basic risk-adjusted costs of capital for each division. First, she estimated the required rate of return on equity, k_s, by using the Security Market Line (SML) equation:

$$k_s = k_{RF} + (k_M - k_{RF})\beta.$$

Here k_M is the return on an "average" stock, k_{RF} is the riskless rate, b is the stock's (or division's) beta coefficient, and the term $(k_M - k_{RF})\beta$ is the stock's (or division's) risk premium above the risk-free rate. Using the current Government of Canada bond rate as the riskless rate, $k_{RF} = 9.0\%$, and a national firm of investment dealers' estimate of the long-run return on the market, $k_M = 14.5\%$, Lam concluded that the corporate cost of equity for Claremont is 14.0 percent:

$$
\begin{aligned}
k_s &= 9.0\% + (14.5\% - 9.0\%)0.9 \\
&= 9.0\% + (5.5\%)0.9 \\
&= 13.95\% \approx 14.0\%.
\end{aligned}
$$

Under current procedures, this 14 percent would be averaged with the cost of debt to find the corporate weighted average cost of capital (WACC), which would then be used to evaluate all projects in all divisions. However, Lam feels that the data clearly show that each division's cost of equity differs from the 14.0 percent corporate cost, depending on the division's own beta.

The next question Lam must consider is capital structure: should different divisions be assigned different capital structures and debt costs, or should they be assigned the corporate average? If different capital structures are to be used, how should they be derived? What interest rate should be used for debt? How should divisional equity costs be adjusted to reflect varying capital structures?

Lam decided to use the corporate target capital structure of 45 percent debt for each division for the following reasons:

(1)   Her old finance professor once argued that the WACC is not very sensitive to capital structure over a fairly wide range of debt ratios; therefore, the issue is not as critical as it might first appear.

(2)   If a division were assigned a high debt ratio, its costs of debt and equity would rise, and this would tend to offset the greater use of lower-cost debt capital.

(3)   She reasoned that she was already going to have a hard time persuading management to accept multiple hurdle rates, and the simpler her approach, the greater her chance of success.

Now that Lam has cost of equity estimates for each division, as well as the appropriate capital structure weights, she can calculate benchmark hurdle rates for each division. Claremont's before-tax cost of debt is currently estimated at 11.0 percent, and the firm has a 40 percent federal-plus-provincial marginal tax rate.

When Lam presented her initial ideas at the first committee meeting, the representative from the Real Estate Division voiced a strong objection. Charlene Lewicki, the division's vice-president, was displeased with the fact that a uniform capital structure of 45 percent debt was proposed. She argued that firms in the real estate industry averaged close to 75 percent debt, and even the most conservative ones used about 60 percent debt, and, based on the conservative firms' bond ratings, their before-tax cost of debt averaged only 10.5 percent, or 50 basis points below Claremont's overall cost of debt. Their cost of equity, using beta coefficients provided by several financial services companies, is about 13.0 percent, which, assuming a tax rate of 40 percent, results in a hurdle rate of about 9.0 percent:

$$WACC = k_a = w_d\ (k_d)\ (1 - T) + w_s\ (k_s)$$
$$= 0.6(10.5\%)(0.6) + 0.4(13.0\%) = 8.98\% \approx 9.0\%.$$

Lewicki argued that if she is forced to use a higher hurdle rate while competing firms use 9.0 percent, Claremont will lose ground in the real estate business. Ken Godfrey backed her up, noting that he had recently attended a conference at which a case study was used involving Fairway Foods Corporation's problem in setting divisional hurdle rates. The restaurant industry tends to have debt ratios of about 70 percent, compared with 35 percent for the major divisions of Fairway Foods. Fairway decided to use a 70 percent debt ratio for its restaurant division, and also a relatively high debt ratio for the toy division, so that comparability with stand-alone competitors could be achieved. Other attendees had pointed out that Apex Steel Company's Equipment Lease Financing Division also has a high debt ratio (about 80 percent debt, as opposed to 33 percent for its other divisions). In both situations, the companies indicated that they could remain competitive only if their divisions could follow industry practice for capital structure when calculating hurdle rates.

When Godfrey finished, Helen Findley noted that both the restaurant and equipment leasing industries have recently been experiencing financial difficulties. Regarding Fairway, Findley cited the following quote from *The Business Daily*:

> Fairway Foods Corporation disclosed some more bad news about its earnings, and it received some bad news itself from a major credit service, which reduced the rating on the food processor's debentures . . . net income fell 27% while sales rose 16% . . . debentures were downgraded to B++ from A+ because of the "continuing deterioration in earnings and fixed charge coverage."

Findley then suggested that these problems might have been brought on in part by an overexpansion resulting from the use of hurdle rates that were unrealistically low. Others agreed with her point, but no conclusions were reached at the meeting; the study group decided to defer action until Lam's report was finalized.

After the meeting, Lam had extended discussions with operating personnel regarding various ways of accounting for individual project risk. She concluded that any system would necessarily be somewhat arbitrary and imprecise. Most individual projects are parts of larger processes, and the results of a given capital project are highly sensitive to market and production conditions for the product. Still, experienced operating personnel admitted that they are more confident about the projected cash flows from some projects than from others, and they recognized that some projects are simply riskier than others. Also, Godfrey reported that some operating personnel have better "track records" in forecasting cash flows than others have, and he takes this fact into account in his own assessment of project risk.

For large projects, generally those involving entirely new technologies or product lines, Jean Lam believes that Monte Carlo simulation or scenario analysis should be used to generate distributions of rates of return. Probabilities would be assigned to sales prices, sales quantity, and so on, and both an expected rate of return and the standard deviation of returns would be developed. However, the vast majority of proposed capital projects would not be subjected to such analyses. Lam feels that the costs would outweigh the benefits of such approaches for smaller projects, especially in view of the highly subjective nature of the estimation process that would have to be used for the probability data.

Still, Lam recommended that divisional managers be required to classify projects into three groups: high risk, average risk, and low risk. Risky projects would be evaluated at a hurdle rate 1.2 times the divisional rate; average projects would be evaluated at the divisional rate; and low-risk projects would be evaluated at a hurdle rate 0.9 times the divisional rate. When this part of the report was taken up at the next study group meeting, the members agreed that the recommended procedure was arbitrary, but most felt that it would be superior to what was currently being done. Moreover, they could suggest no better procedure.

In drafting her final conclusions, Lam remained convinced that capital budgeting must involve judgement as well as quantitative analyses. The current capital budgeting process is as follows: (1) one hurdle rate is used throughout the entire corporation; (2) NPVs, IRRs, MIRRs, and paybacks are calculated; and (3) these quantitative data are used, along with such qualitative factors as "what the project does for our strategic position in the market," in making the final "accept, reject, or defer" decision. Lam's report emphasized that this general procedure should be followed, but that the quantitative inputs used in the final decision would be better if differential risk-adjusted discount rates were used.

The day before her final report was due, Jean Lam received a call for jury duty. She had avoided serving the last two times she was called, so there was no way out this time—it was jury duty or jail for contempt of court. Assume that you have been assigned to take over the task of completing the report and defending it before the study group. Lam did leave you with the following list of questions to help you complete the task. She also informed you that Phillip Calhoun, the financial VP, was thinking about giving you a significant promotion, but that your chances for the promotion will be ruined if you don't do a good job writing up the report and then answering questions about it.

Questions

1. Estimate the divisional hurdle rates for each division. Assume for this purpose that all divisions use a 45 percent debt ratio.

2. Now assume that, within divisions, projects are identified as being high risk, average risk, or low risk. What hurdle rates would be assigned to projects in those risk categories within each division?

3. How comfortable are you with the 1.2 and 0.9 project risk adjustment factors? Is there a theoretical foundation for the size of these adjustments?

4. Suppose the Ceramic Coatings Division has an exceptionally large number of projects whose returns exceed the risk-adjusted hurdle rates, so its growth rate substantially exceeds the corporate average. What effect would this have, over time, on Claremont's corporate beta and on its overall cost of capital? (Assume that the aggregate risk of the division remains unchanged.)

5. Suppose that, despite the higher cost of capital for risky projects (1.2 times divisional cost), the Equipment Manufacturing Division made relatively heavy investments in projects deemed to be more risky than average. What effect would this have on the firm's corporate beta and its overall cost of capital? How long would it take for the effects of these relatively risky investments to show up in the corporate beta as reported by brokers and investment advisory services?

6. Do you agree with Lam on the capital structure issue? How would your thinking be affected if (a) each division raised its own debt, that is, if the divisions were set up as wholly-owned subsidiaries, which then issued their own debt (in fact, Claremont raises debt capital at the corporate level, and funds are then made available by headquarters to the various divisions); (b) divisions issued their own debt, but the corporation guaranteed the divisional debt; or (c) all debt was issued by the corporation (which is actually the case)?

7. One problem with a market risk analysis such as the one Lam is conducting relates to differences in reported market beta coefficients. Some services calculate and report straight historical betas, while others make adjustments for the tendency of betas to approach 1.0 over time. A few

services even attempt to include fundamental economic factors in their beta calculations. Explain why reported beta values (even pure historical betas) are so inconsistent. Do historical betas provide good measures of the future riskiness of firms (or divisions)?

8. Lam's analysis requires that betas be estimated for Claremont's four divisions, and she used both the pure play and the accounting beta methods for these estimates. Suppose she did not feel comfortable with beta analysis. Could divisional (and project) hurdle rates be established using total risk analysis? If so, describe how this might be done. (Hint: The risk of divisions (and projects) can be viewed on a stand-alone basis or on a within-firm basis, which treats the firm as a portfolio of assets.)

9. Claremont, like most companies, uses an incentive-based compensation plan for its upper management personnel. Under its plan, division managers receive approximately half of their annual compensation, on average, as bonuses or incentive stock. These percentages vary greatly, of course, from year to year, depending on the state of the economy and on how both the corporation and the divisions did during the recent past. The incentive compensation at the division level is based on three factors: (1) the division's ROE, (2) its sales growth, and (3) its earnings growth, all averaged over the last 3 years. The incentive compensation of the senior corporate executives is based on the same three factors, but measured for the entire corporation.

   a. Do you see any obvious conceptual problems with the company's compensation program?

   b. How would you expect the compensation plan to influence managers' reactions to Lam's recommendations? Would these reactions be good or bad from the standpoint of maximizing the price of Claremont's stock?

   c. Should Claremont change either the compensation plan or its capital budgeting procedures to make them more consistent with one another and with the goal of stock price maximization?

III

Capital Structure

Case 5
Financial Leverage Floral Designs, Inc.

Case 6
Capital Structure Policy Canola Copiers, Incorporated

5

---

*Financial
Leverage*

Floral Designs, Inc.

Floral Designs, Inc., a producer of high-quality artificial flowers, was founded in 1981 by Lise Doucette, president and chief executive officer, and Michelle Weber, senior vice-president. In 1980, when Doucette was working on her PhD in materials science, she discovered a way to use acetate cloth to make a new type of artificial flower. Flower petals and leaves could be formed from acetate cloth that had been treated with a plastic resin, allowing the individual piece to retain its shape and durability, but still have the texture and feel of silk. Doucette developed a prototype, and she then asked several florists to evaluate the product. The production cost of the acetate flowers was less than one-fourth the cost of high-quality silk flowers, yet the two were virtually indistinguishable, so the florists were quite enthusiastic. With the strong endorsement of the florists, Doucette abandoned plans for a teaching career and teamed up with Weber, who had strong financial and managerial talents, to form Floral Designs, Inc. Doucette currently owns 30 percent of the stock, Weber owns 25 percent, other employees own 10 percent, and the remaining 35 percent is held by the public and trades in the over-the-counter market.

Although the company has experienced reasonable growth, Doucette and Weber do not think they have even scratched the surface of the potential market for high-quality artificial flowers. Further, in early 1990, Doucette developed a new and revolutionary production method for manufacturing certain types of acetate flowers. With the new process, it will be possible to form the very complex shapes required for artificial peonies, hyacinths, dahlias, and other flowers with small, curved petals. These flowers are very popular in live arrangements, but moulded plastic imitations are not of high enough quality to permit florists to use them in artificial bouquets. Even silk facsimiles have never achieved the same degree of realism that has been possible with less complex flowers such as roses, orchids, and lilies. Also, the labour required to produce silk versions of small-petalled artificial flowers has made them too expensive for most applications.

Table 1
1991 Sales Estimates for Floral Designs' New Acetate Flowers

Probability	Unit Sales (in Gross)
0.1	80 000
0.2	110 000
0.4	150 000
0.2	190 000
0.1	220 000

Production tests for the new process have been completed, so the only uncertainty about the economics of the new production system is associated with the demand for the flowers. The traditional market for high-quality artificial flowers consists mainly of florists and professional flower arrangers, although some are sold to individuals through decorators and high-price boutiques. Many individuals do buy plastic artificial flowers for various uses, but the acetate flowers would be more expensive than the plastic kind, even if they were made with the new high-volume production system. So, there is a real question as to the demand for the new flowers.

Despite the uncertainty over the ultimate market for the acetate flowers as reflected in Table 1, Doucette and Weber are committed to shifting to the new production system. Further, they have concluded that since plant expansion is necessary to implement the new system, the firm should expand now to meet the future growth requirements that are likely to occur as more and more individuals enter the demand side of the market. The projected total capital outlay, plus the additional working capital needed, requires a $13 million increase in total assets during 1991.

The new production method will involve fixed costs of $3.5 million per year and variable costs of $150 per gross (12 dozen, or 144, flowers). The estimated sales price is $200 per gross, or roughly $1.39 per flower. Although this is three times the cost of regular plastic flowers, it is still less than one-fourth the price of high-quality silk replicas.

To finance the expansion, Floral Designs can use bonds, common stock, or some combination of the two. The board of directors—but in reality, Doucette and Weber—now have to make the final decision about the financing method. In a recent directors' meeting, two views were presented. One director, D.B. Reznick, chairman of the board of Canadian Securities Inc., an investment dealer that makes a market in Floral Designs' stock, strongly recommends that the company choose debt financing at this time. Reznick believes that inflation is likely to increase significantly in the next few years as the falling dollar makes imports more and more expensive, and that debt incurred now can be repaid in the future with "cheap dollars." Reznick says his discussions with the company's stockholders (Reznick's firm has many customers who own Floral Designs stock) suggest that the investing public is currently more interested in companies that are willing to use leverage than in conservative firms. He also notes that most investors hold diversified portfolios, which minimizes the risk on any one stock, so this increases their willingness to assume more risk on an individual security.

Charles Davis, vice-president of Provincial Trust Company, takes the opposite point of view. He argues that the firm's risk will be increased too much if it sells additional debt at this time. Davis maintains that although the sales forecasts are favourable, the cost of getting the new process installed and operating could be higher than anticipated, or sales could fall below the anticipated level, in which case the company could be in serious trouble. Davis also notes that his company has frequently mentioned the debt ratio as a measure of corporate strength. He adds that investors' aversion to risk generally results in lower stock prices for companies with high debt ratios. Davis also stresses that if the company uses additional common stock now, its financial position will be strong, and if demand should exceed expectations, requiring new facilities in the near future, the company would be in an excellent position to sell debt at a later date. Finally, Davis states that his bank's economists believe that interest rates will soon fall, so, if the company defers debt financing, it may be able to obtain debt at an even lower cost in the future.

Table 2

Financial Statements of Floral Designs, Inc.

Income Statement for Years Ended June 31
(Thousands of Dollars)

	1989	1990
Sales	$32 000	$40 000
Total costs (excluding interest)	20 899	25 500
Earnings before interest and tax (EBIT)	$11 101	$14 500
Interest on long-term debt	630	900
Earnings before tax	$10 471	$13 600
Tax (40 percent)	4 188	5 440
Net income	$ 6 283	$ 8 160

Balance Sheet for Years Ended June 31
(Thousands of Dollars)

	1989	1990
Current assets	$12 850	$13 500
Net fixed assets	8 950	14 500
Other assets	5 200	7 000
Total assets	$27 000	$35 000
Current liabilities	$ 4 500	$ 6 480
Long-term debt (9 percent)	7 000	10 000
Common stock, $2.50 par value	5 000	5 000
Retained earnings	10 500	13 520
Total claims	$27 000	$35 000

The currently outstanding long-term debt (see Table 2) carries a 9 percent interest rate. Because the general level of interest rates is higher now than it was when the old debt was issued, the new debt would carry a higher rate. A "poison put" provision in the contract for the presently outstanding debt states that it must be retired (at par) at the holders' option before any new long-term debt can be issued, if the new debt carries a rate of interest above 9 percent. At the directors' meeting, Reznick indicated that this provision would present no problem because the company would be able to raise enough new debt to provide funds for the expansion and also to pay off the old debt.

Another clause in the debt contract states that there is a 20 percent prepayment penalty for repaying the debt ahead of schedule, unless it is refunded with higher-cost debt. Thus, Floral Designs is effectively precluded from reducing its long-term debt below $10 million.

When Doucette and Weber pressed Reznick and Davis for information on how increasing the debt ratio would affect the price/earnings ratio, there was some disagreement. Davis thought that the current price/earnings ratio of 6.5 would decline, while Reznick believed that Floral Designs' investors would not be averse to a higher debt level, so the current P/E would not change.

A $13 million increase in total assets will be required to implement the new production process, and the investment dealers have indicated that debt would be available according to the following schedule. The rates shown are not marginal rates in the sense that each is applied just to its respective increment; rather, the rates are applied to the entire amount of debt issued. For example, if the firm borrows $15 million, the interest cost on the entire amount would be 13 percent. Also, remember that the $10 million of outstanding 9 percent debt must be retired if the company chooses to use additional debt.

Amount Borrowed	Interest Rate
$ 7.01 to $11 million	11.50%
11.01 to 14 million	12.25
14.01 to 17 million	13.00
17.01 to 20 million	14.00
20.01 to 23 million	16.00

The matter of the P/E ratio was especially troubling to Davis, so he consulted with several investment dealers for their opinions. Based on these conversations, he concluded that the following schedule is applicable:

LT Debt /Assets	P/E
up to 30%	6.5
30.1 – 36%	5.5
36.1 – 45%	5.0
45.1 – 50%	4.5

The debt/assets ratios shown here do not include current liabilities; they relate only to long-term debt. If short-term debt were included, the data would not be materially different. Davis sent the figures to Weber and asked her to take them into account before reaching a decision.

Doucette and Weber concluded that Weber should prepare a report for presentation at the next directors' meeting. Now she asks you, her assistant, to help with the report by answering the following questions. A partially completed worksheet is provided in Table 3 to help you with some of the questions.

Questions

1. Calculate expected earnings per share and stock prices at capital structures of $10, $11, $14, $17, $20, and $23 million of long-term debt. Assume a 30 percent growth rate from 1990 to 1991 in EBIT from existing operations, and combine this projected 1991 "assets-in-place" EBIT with the expected incremental EBIT resulting from the new expansion. Floral Designs expects that its federal-plus-provincial tax rate for 1991 and the foreseeable future will be 40 percent. Also, assume that any funds not raised by debt will be raised by selling common stock at a net price of $20 per share ($25 price to the public less a $5 per share flotation cost.) Which capital structure alternative would you recommend? (Hint: Consider stock price maximization as the firm's primary goal and use Table 3 as a guide.)

2. Use data from your answer to Question 1, and suppose the optimal amount of debt is raised in the form of a 20-year amortized term loan. What would the annual amortization payment be? Use this value to calculate the debt service coverage ratio for 1991.

3. What is Floral Designs' expected rate of return on common equity at the optimal capital structure? (The expected rate of return on equity is equal to the expected net income available to common stockholders divided by total common equity.)

4. Assume that Floral Designs plans to pay out all earnings as dividends and thus to have a zero growth rate, and that investors are aware of this. What value for k_s is implied at the optimal capital structure?

5. If Doucette and Weber, and the other board members, had only a small stock ownership, might their financing decision be influenced by whether their compensation consisted entirely of a fixed salary or included a substantial element in the form of stock options? Explain, and answer more in general terms than in relation to the data in the case.

6. Suppose the cost of the expansion is uncertain, and could run as high as $20 million, well above the original estimate of $13 million. How would this possibility affect your recommendation? If you are using the *Lotus* model for this case, calculate the expected stock price for each capital structure, assuming a $20 million cost of expansion.

7. Suppose Reznick is correct, and the P/E ratio actually would remain at the current level even if the debt ratio were increased up to the limits given in the case. How would this affect the expected outcome?

8. Based on the information given in the case, does it appear that the investing public is aware of the plans for the new process? What difference would it make if the public knew or did not know of the new situation? If the public was not informed, would it be to the company's advantage to try to inform them? If so, how could the information be conveyed? If any of the board members had some extra money, would you recommend that they purchase the company's stock on the open market at this time?

9. No mention of the capital asset pricing model (CAPM) was made in the case because the CAPM was not considered in the actual decision. Explain how CAPM concepts might have been employed in the analysis. Be sure to discuss how financial leverage would affect the firm's beta coefficient and hence the firm's cost of equity and value.

10. Remember that Doucette and Weber each own a substantial amount of the outstanding stock (assume that this stock represents essentially all of their personal net worths). What impact does potential loss of control have on the capital structure decision?

11. The analysis used in the case extended only one year into the future. To look further into the future, what additional information would you need? Based on the (very limited) information about the extended future given in the case, do you think it likely that projections for the future might alter the conclusions you reached?

Table 3
Selected Case Data
(in Thousands Except per Share Data)

Amount of new debt	$ 0	$11 000	$14 000	$17 000	$20 000	$23 000
Cost of LT debt	9.00%	11.50%	X	X	X	16.00%
Existing debt	$10 000	0	X	X	X	$ 0
Total LT debt	$10 000	X	X	X	X	$23 000
1991 total assets	$48 000	X	X	X	X	$48 000
1991 LT debt ratio at book value	20.83%	22.92%	X	X	X	X
P/E ratio	6.5	6.5	X	X	X	X
New common stock required	$13 000	$12 000	X	X	X	$ 0
Net price/share	$ 20	$ 20	X	X	X	$ 20
New shares required	650	X	X	X	X	0
Existing shares	2 000	X	X	X	X	2 000
Total shares outstanding	2 650	X	X	X	X	X
1991 forecasted EBIT	$22 850	X	X	X	X	$22 850
Interest expense	900	X	X	X	X	3 680
Taxable income	$21 950	$21 585	X	X	X	X
Taxes	8 780	8 634	X	X	X	X
Net income	$13 170	X	X	X	X	$11 502
Shares outstanding	2 650	X	X	X	X	2 000
EPS	$ 4.97	X	X	X	X	X
P/E ratio	6.5	X	X	X	X	X
1991 stock price	$ 32.30	X	X	$ 29.61	X	X
Amortization payment	$ 1 095	$ 1 427	X	X	X	X
Interest component	$ 900	$ 1 265	X	X	X	X
Grossed-up principal	$ 326	$ 270	X	X	X	X
Forecasted coverage	18.6	14.9	X	X	X	X
Forecasted TIE ratio	25.4	18.1	X	X	X	X
Forecasted ROE	41.78%	42.43%	X	X	X	X

6

Capital Structure
Policy

Canola Copiers, Incorporated

Canola Copiers, Inc., franchises small copying and print shops to independent dealers throughout Canada. Basically, the franchisee buys the exclusive right to use the Canola Copiers name within a given territory, and also receives marketing and management support from Canola Copiers. Additionally, copy machines can be leased from Canola Copiers under relatively favourable terms, since the firm purchases them in large quantities. Supplies such as paper and toner can also be purchased directly from Canola Copiers at substantial savings.

The company was founded in 1975 by Bill MacIntosh, then a student in Toronto, who recognized that the country virtually ran on paper. Canola Copiers expanded rapidly from its base in Toronto, first by opening stores at different locations across southern Ontario and then by franchising into other parts of the country. Bill was a firm believer in the virtues of equity financing. Although the company had issued debt periodically, especially to finance company-owned store expansion, Bill always used Canola Copiers' cash flows to retire the debt as soon as possible. Recent growth has involved franchising, where the franchisee puts up the required capital, and hence there has been no need for outside capital for several years.

Bill believes that the market for his stores has finally matured. First, numerous competing chains have appeared on the scene, and it seems that every town in the country with a population over 5000 now has at least one fast-food and one copy-centre franchise. Second, many formerly good customers are now buying laser printers or copy machines, or both, and doing their copy work in house. Thus, Canola Copiers expects its 1990 EBIT of $30 000 000 to remain relatively constant into the future.

Canola Copiers has 10 000 000 shares of common stock outstanding, and they are traded in the over-the-counter market. The current share price is $12, so the total value of the equity is $120 million. The book value of the assets is also $120 million, so the stock now sells at its book value. Canola Copiers' federal-plus-provincial tax rate is 40 percent. Bill owns 20 percent of the outstanding stock, and others in the management group own an additional 10 percent. Bill's financial manager, Greg Vanderveen, has been preaching for years that Canola Copiers should use debt in its capital structure. "After all," says Greg, "everybody else is using debt like there's no tomorrow—look at the growth of the junk-bond market. Also, underleveraged companies are terribly exposed to hostile takeovers." Bill's reaction to Greg's prodding was cautious, but Bill was willing to give Greg the chance to "prove" his point.

Greg had worked with Bill for the past 6 years, and he knew that the only way he could convince Bill that the firm should use debt financing was to conduct a comprehensive analysis. To begin, Greg arranged for a joint meeting with his former finance professor and an investment dealer who specializes in corporate financing for service companies. After several hours, the trio agreed on these estimates for the relationship between the use of debt financing and Canola Copiers' capital costs:

Amount Borrowed	Cost of Debt	Cost of Equity
$ 0	–	15.0%
25 000 000	10.0%	15.5
50 000 000	11.0	16.5
75 000 000	13.0	18.0
100 000 000	16.0	20.0
125 000 000	20.0	25.0

If Canola Copiers were to recapitalize, the borrowed funds would be used to repurchase stock in the open market. Now Greg must write a question-and-answer working paper that he can present to Bill MacIntosh to "sell" the idea of using financial leverage. Help him by answering the following questions.

Questions

1. What is the difference between business risk and financial risk? How can these risks be measured in a total risk sense? How can they be measured in a market risk framework? How does business risk affect capital structure decisions?

2. Although Canola Copiers' EBIT is expected to be $30 000 000, there is a great deal of uncertainty in the estimate, as indicated by the following probability distribution:

Probability	EBIT
0.25	$10 000 000
0.50	30 000 000
0.25	50 000 000

Now assume that Canola Copiers had only two capitalization alternatives: either an all-equity capital structure with $120 000 000 of stock, or $60 000 000 of 12 percent debt plus $60 000 000 of equity.

  a. Construct partial income statements for each financing alternative at each EBIT level. (Hint: Use the upper half of Table 1 as a guide.)

  b. Now calculate the ROE and TIE ratios for each alternative at each EBIT level.

  c. Finally, discuss the risk/return tradeoffs under the two financing alternatives. In your discussion, consider the expected ROE and the standard deviation of ROE under each alternative.

3. Now consider the impact of leverage on Canola Copiers' overall value and share price. Since Canola Copiers is not expected to grow, Greg believes that the following equations can be used in the analysis:

  (1) $S = [\text{EBIT} - k_d(D)](1 - T)/k_s$.
  (2) $V = S + D$.
  (3) $P = (V - D_0)/n_0$
  (4) $n_1 = n_0 - D/P$.

Here

S = market value of equity.
EBIT = earnings before interest and taxes.
k_d = cost of debt.
D = market (and book) value of new debt.
D_0 = market value of old debt.
T = tax rate.
k_s = cost of equity.
V = total market value.
P = stock price after recapitalization.
n_0 = number of shares before recapitalization.
n_1 = number of shares after recapitalization.

  a. Explain in words the logic of Equation 1 for a zero-growth firm.

  b. Describe briefly, without using numbers, the sequence of events that would occur if Canola Copiers decided to recapitalize.

4. Now assume that Canola Copiers does recapitalize.

  a. Estimate Canola Copiers' stock price with and without debt. (Hint: Use the lower half of Table 1 as a guide.)

b. How many shares would remain after recapitalization under each scenario?

c. Considering only the six levels of debt proposed in the case, what is Canola Copiers' optimal capital structure?

5. Now assume that Canola Copiers recapitalized with $25 000 000 of debt, and hence $S = \$106\,451\,613$, $D = \$25\,000\,000$, $V = \$131\,451\,613$, $P = \$13.15$, and $n = 8\,098\,160$.

   a. What would Canola Copiers' share price and ending number of shares be if it increased its debt to $50 000 000 by issuing $50 000 000 of new debt and using half to refund the existing issue and half to repurchase stock? (Assume that the indenture for the existing debt prohibits Canola Copiers from issuing additional debt without refunding.)

   b. Now assume that Canola Copiers issues $25 000 000 of new debt without refunding the existing issue. What would be the stock price and ending number of shares in this situation? (Assume that the old and the new debt issues have the same priority of claims. Also, remember that if the firm has $50 million of debt, its cost of debt is 11 percent, so the new $25 million debt issue will have an interest rate of 11 percent.)

   c. Explain why the prices are higher in Parts a and b than those obtained in Question 4.

6. Managers are also concerned with the impact of financial leverage on the firm's EPS and weighted-average cost of capital (WACC).

   a. Calculate the EPS at each debt level, assuming that Canola Copiers begins with zero debt and raises new debt in a single issue.

   b. Is EPS maximized at the same debt level that maximizes stock price?

   c. Calculate the WACC at each debt level.

   d. What is the relationship between the stock price and the WACC?

7. Consider what would happen if Canola Copiers' business risk were considerably different from that used to estimate the financial leverage/capital cost relationships given in the case.

   a. Describe in words how the analysis would change if Canola Copiers' business risk were significantly higher than originally estimated. If you are using the *Lotus* model for this case, assume that the following set of leverage/cost estimates hold:

Amount Borrowed	Cost of Debt	Cost of Equity
$ 0	–	16.0%
25 000 000	11.0%	17.0
50 000 000	13.0	19.0
75 000 000	16.0	22.0
100 000 000	20.0	26.0
125 000 000	25.0	31.0

What is the optimal capital structure in this situation?

b. How would things change if the firm's business risk were considerably lower than originally estimated? If you are using the *Lotus* model for this case, assume that the following set of leverage/cost estimates hold:

Amount Borrowed	Cost of Debt	Cost of Equity
$ 0	–	14.0%
25 000 000	9.0%	14.3
50 000 000	9.5	15.0
75 000 000	10.5	16.0
100 000 000	12.5	17.5
125 000 000	15.5	20.0

What is the optimal capital structure in this situation?

8. How would control issues affect the capital structure decision?

9. Briefly discuss the practicality of the analysis.

a. What are the major weaknesses of the type of analysis called for in the case?

b. What other approaches could managers use to help determine an appropriate target capital structure? Is the target capital structure best thought of as a point estimate or as a range?

c. What other factors should managers consider when setting target capital structures?

Table 1
Selected Case Data

ROE and TIE Analysis

Total assets	$120 000 000
Debt used	$ 60 000 000
Cost of debt	12%
Equity amount	$ 60 000 000

	All Equity			50% Debt		
Probability	0.25	0.50	0.25	0.25	0.50	0.25
EBIT	$10 000 000	$30 000 000	$50 000 000	$10 000 000	$30 000 000	$50 000 000
Interest	0	0	0	7 200 000	7 200 000	7 200 000
EBT	$10 000 000	X	X	$ 2 800 000	$22 800 000	$42 800 000
Taxes	4 000 000	X	X	1 120 000	9 120 000	17 120 000
Net income	X	$18 000 000	$30 000 000	$ 1 680 000	$13 680 000	$25 680 000
ROE	5.0	%	25.0 %	2.8 %	22.8	%
TIE	n.a.	X	n.a.	1.39	4.17	X
E(ROE)		n.a.%			X	X
Std dev ROE		15.0%			14.1	
CV		7.1			0.62%	
		0.47				

Valuation Analysis

D (000)s	S	V	D/V	P	WACC	Number of Shares	EPS
$ 0	$120 000 000	$120 000 000	0%	$12.00	15.0%	10 000 000	$1.80
25 000	106 451 613	131 451 613	19	13.15	13.7	8 098 160	2.04
50 000	X	X	X	X	X	X	X
75 000	X	X	X	X	X	X	X
100 000	42 000 000	142 000 000	70	14.20	12.7	2 957 746	2.84
125 000	12 000 000	137 000 000	91	13.70	13.1	875 912	3.43

IV

Capital Budgeting

Case 7
Capital Budgeting Decision Methods Clarke Controls

Case 8
Cash Flow Estimation McReath Corporation (A)

Case 9
Risk Analysis in Capital Budgeting McReath Corporation (B)

Case 10
Capital Budgeting with Staged Entry Computer-ese Incorporated

7

*Capital Budgeting
Decision Methods*

Clarke Controls

Although he was hired as a financial analyst, Kenneth O'Connor's first assignment at Clarke Controls was with the firm's marketing department. Historically, the major focus of Clarke's sales effort was on demonstrating the technological superiority of the firm's product line. However, many of Clarke's traditional customers have embarked on cost-cutting programs in recent years, and as a result, Clarke's marketing director asked O'Connor's boss, the financial VP, to lend O'Connor to marketing to help them develop some analytical procedures for the sales force to use to demonstrate the financial benefits of buying Clarke's products.

Clarke Controls manufactures fluid control systems that are used in a wide variety of applications, including sewage treatment systems, petroleum refining, and pipeline transmission. The complete systems include sophisticated pumps, sensors, and control units that continuously monitor the flow rate and the pressure along a line, and automatically adjust the pump to meet preset pressure specifications. Most of Clarke's systems are made up of standard components, and most complete systems are priced from $50 000 to $100 000. Because of the highly technical nature of the products, the majority of Clarke's sales people have backgrounds in engineering.

As he began to think about his assignment, Kenneth quickly came to the conclusion that the best way to "sell" a system to a cost-conscious customer would be to conduct a capital budgeting analysis that would demonstrate the system's cost effectiveness. Further, Kenneth concluded that the best way to begin was with an analysis for one of Clarke's actual customers.

From discussions with the firm's sales people, O'Connor concluded that a proposed sale to Superior Chemical Company was perfect to use as an illustration. Superior is considering the purchase of one of Clarke's standard fluid control systems, which costs $80 000, including taxes and delivery. It would cost Superior another $5000 to install the equipment, and this expense would be added to the invoice price of the equipment to determine the capital cost of the system. The system is a Class 10 asset (Capital Cost Allowance [CCA] Rate = 30%). After 8 years, the system's salvage value is estimated to be equal to the Undepreciated Capital Cost (UCC) at that time.

This system would replace a control system that has been used for about 20 years and that has been fully depreciated. The costs for removing the current system are about equal to its scrap value, so its current net market value is zero.

The advantages of the new system are (1) that it would be more energy efficient; (2) that it would reduce waste, because the chemical processes could be more carefully controlled; and (3) that fewer workers would be required to monitor and maintain it. In total, the new system would save Superior $25 000 annually in before-tax operating costs. For capital budgeting, Superior uses a 10 percent cost of capital, and its federal-plus-provincial tax rate is 40 percent.

Lynn Gorman, Clarke's marketing manager, gave Kenneth a free hand in structuring the analysis, but with one exception—she told him to include the modified IRR (MIRR) as one of the decision criteria. To calculate MIRR, all of the cash inflows are compounded to the terminal year, in this case Year 8, at the project's cost of capital, and then these compounded values are summed to produce the project's terminal value. Then, MIRR is found as the discount rate that causes the present value of the terminal value to equal the net cost of the equipment. Gorman had recently attended a seminar on capital budgeting, and, according to the seminar leader, the MIRR method has significant advantages over the use of the regular IRR, and for that reason it is rapidly replacing IRR as a primary capital budgeting method.

Now put yourself in Kenneth's position, and develop a capital budgeting analysis for the fluid control systems. As you go through the analysis, keep in mind that since the purpose of the analysis is to help Clarke's sales representatives sell equipment to other nonfinancial people, the analysis must be as clear as possible, yet technically correct. In other words, the analysis must not only be right, it must also be understandable to decision makers. In addition, the presenter—Kenneth, in this case—must be able to answer all questions, ranging from the performance characteristics of the equipment to the assumptions underlying the capital budgeting decision criteria.

Questions

1. Table 1 contains the complete cash flow analysis. Examine it carefully, and be prepared to answer any questions that might be posed. What are the project's incremental cash flows in each year?
2. What is the project's NPV? Explain the economic rationale behind the NPV. Could the NPV of this particular project be different for Superior Chemical Company than for one of Clarke's other potential customers? Explain.

Table 1
Project Net Cash Flows

Year	Net Cost	CCA Tax Saving	After-Tax Cost Saving	Terminal Cash Flow	Net Cash Flow
0	($85 000)				($85 000)
1		$5 100	15 000		20 100
2		8 670	15 000		23 670
3		6 069	15 000		21 069
4		4 248	15 000		19 248
5		2 974	15 000		17 974
6		2 082	15 000		17 082
7		1 457	15 000		16 457
8		1 020	15 000	5950	21 970

3. Calculate the proposed project's IRR. Explain the rationale for using the IRR to evaluate capital investment projects. Could the IRR for this project be different for Superior than for another customer? Explain.

4. Suppose one of Superior's executives uses the payback method as a primary capital budgeting decision tool and wants some payback information.
   a. What is the project's payback period?
   b. What is the rationale behind the use of payback as a project evaluation tool?
   c. What deficiencies does payback have as a capital budgeting decision method?
   d. Does payback provide any useful information regarding capital budgeting decisions?
   e. Clarke Controls has a number of different types of products—some that are relatively expensive and some that are inexpensive, and some that have very long lives and some with short lives. Strictly as a sales tool, without regard to the validity of the analysis, would the payback be of more help to the sales staff for some types of equipment than for others? Explain.
   f. People occasionally find the payback, then take its reciprocal, and use the reciprocal as an estimate of the project's rate of return. Would this procedure be more appropriate for projects with very long or short lives? Explain.

5. What is the project's MIRR? What is the conceptual difference between the IRR and the MIRR? Which is better? Why?

6. Suppose a potential customer wants to know the project's profitability index (PI). What is the value of the PI for Superior, and what is the rationale behind this measure?

7. Under what conditions do NPV, IRR, MIRR, and PI all lead to the same accept/reject decision? When can conflicts occur? If a conflict arises, which method should be used, and why?

8. Suppose the control system qualifies for an investment tax credit (ITC). What would be the impact of a 10 percent ITC on the acceptability of the control system project? No calculations are necessary; just discuss the impact.

9. Plot the project's NPV profile and explain how the graph can be used.

10. Now suppose that Clarke also sells a smaller, short-life control system. In a typical installation, the system's cash flows are as follows:

Year	Net Cash Flow
0	($60 000)
1	75 000

Assuming a 10 percent cost of capital, what is this project's NPV, and its IRR? Draw this project's NPV profile on the same graph you drew in Question 9, and then discuss the complete graph. Be sure to talk about (1) mutually exclusive versus independent projects, (2) conflicts between projects, and (3) the effect of the cost of capital on the existence of conflicts. What conditions must exist with respect to timing of cash flows and project size for conflicts to arise?

11. Lynn Gorman informed Kenneth that the sales reps would all have laptop computers, so they could demonstrate the capital budgeting analyses. For example, they could insert data for their client companies into the models and do both the basic analysis and the sensitivity analyses, in which they examine the effects of changes in such things as the annual cost savings, the cost of capital, and the tax rate. Therefore, Kenneth and Lynn developed the following "sensitivity questions," which they plan to go over with the sales representatives:
    a. Suppose the annual cost savings differed from the projected level; how would this affect the various decision criteria? What is the minimum annual cost savings at which the system would be cost justified? Discuss what is happening, and if you are using the *Lotus* model, quantify your answers; otherwise, just discuss the nature of the effects.
    b. Repeat the type of analysis done in Part a, but now vary the cost of capital. Again, quantify your answers if you are using the *Lotus* model.
    c. Repeat the type of analysis done in Part a, but now vary the tax rate. Again, quantify your answers if you are using the *Lotus* model.

    d. Would the capability to do sensitivity analysis on a laptop computer be of much assistance to the sales staff? Can you anticipate any problems that might arise? Explain.

12. Now suppose that Clarke sells another product that is used to speed up the flow through pipelines. However, after a year of use, the pipeline must undergo expensive repairs. In a typical installation, the cash flows of this product might be as follows:

Year	Net Cash Flow
0	($ 20 000)
1	100,000
2	(80 000)

Assuming a 10 percent cost of capital, what are this project's NPV, IRR, and MIRR[1]? Draw this new project's NPV profile on a new graph. Explain what is happening with this project.

---

1 The MIRR is found in three steps: (1) compound all net operating cash inflows forward to the terminal year at the cost of capital; (2) sum the compounded cash inflows to obtain the *terminal value* of the inflows; and (3) find the discount rate that forces the present value of the terminal value to equal the PV of the net investment outlays. This discount rate is defined as the MIRR.

8

McReath Corporation (A)

McReath Corporation is a leading producer of fresh, frozen, and made-from-concentrate peach drinks. The firm was founded in 1922 by Alexander McReath, an army veteran who settled in Toronto, Ontario, after World War I and began selling real estate. Since real estate sales were booming, McReath's fortunes soared. His investment philosophy, which he proudly displayed behind his desk, was "Buy land. They aren't making any more of it." He practised what he preached, and he invested most of his sales commissions in peach groves located along the Niagara Peninsula. Originally, McReath sold his peaches to wholesalers for distribution to grocery stores, but in the 1940s and 1950s, when peach sales were expanding, he joined with several other producers to form McReath Corporation, which then expanded into peach processing. Today, its Sun Joy, Niagara Gold, and Peachy Delite brands are sold throughout Canada.

McReath's management is currently evaluating a new product: all-natural frozen peach desserts. The new product would cost more, but it is superior to the competing frozen desserts in the marketplace. Joanne Engel and Doug Bower, recent business school graduates who are now working at McReath as financial analysts, must analyze this project, along with two other potential investments, and then present their findings to the company's executive committee.

Production facilities for the frozen peach dessert product would be set up in an unused section of McReath's main plant. Relatively inexpensive, used machinery with an estimated cost of only $250 000 would be purchased, but shipping costs to move the machinery to McReath's plant would total $20 000, and installation charges would add another $30 000 to the total equipment cost. Further, McReath's inventories (raw materials, work-in-process, and finished goods) would have to be increased by $10 000 at the time of the initial investment. The machinery has a remaining economic life of 4 years, and is a Class 39 asset; capital cost allowance (CCA) will be claimed at a rate of 12.5% in Year 1 and 25% for Years 2, 3, and 4. The machinery is expected to have a salvage value of $110 742 after 4 years of use, its Undepreciated Capital Cost (UCC) at that time.

The section of the plant where frozen peach dessert production would occur has been unused for several years, and consequently it has suffered some deterioration. Last year, as part of a routine facilities improvement program, McReath spent $100 000 to rehabilitate that section of the main plant. Doug Bower believes that this outlay, which has already been paid and expensed for tax purposes, should be charged to the new peach project. His contention is that if the rehabilitation had not taken place, the firm would have to spend the $100 000 to make the site suitable for McReath's new project.

McReath's management expects to sell 200 000 containers of the new frozen peach dessert in each of the next 4 years, at a price of $2.00 per container, but $1.50 per container would be needed to cover fixed and variable cash operating costs. In examining the sales figures, Joanne Engel noted a short memo from McReath's sales manager that expressed concern that the new peach project would cut into the firm's sales of frozen peach drinks; this type of effect is called an *externality*. Specifically, the sales manager estimated that frozen peach drink sales would fall by 5 percent if frozen peach desserts were introduced. Joanne then talked to both the sales and production managers, and she concluded that the new project would probably lower the firm's frozen peach drinks sales by $20 000 per year, but, at the same time, it would also reduce production costs for this product by $10 000 per year, all on a pre-tax basis. Thus, the net externality effect would be −$20 000 + $10 000 = −$10 000. McReath's federal-plus-provincial tax rate is 40 percent, and its overall cost of capital is 10 percent, calculated as follows:

$$WACC = w_d k_d (1 - T) + w_s k_s$$
$$= 0.5(8\%)(0.6) + 0.5(15.2\%)$$
$$= 10.0\%.$$

Joanne and Doug were asked to analyze the project, and then to present their findings in a "tutorial" manner to McReath's executive committee. The financial vice-president, Joanne and Doug's supervisor, wants them to educate some of the other executives, especially the marketing and sales managers, in the theory of capital budgeting so that these executives will have a better understanding of his capital budgeting decisions. Therefore, Joanne and Doug have decided to ask and then answer a series of questions as set forth below. Specifics on the other two projects that must be analyzed are provided in Questions 11 and 12.

Questions

1. Define the term "incremental cash flow," and then set forth the frozen peach dessert project's operating cash flow statement for the first year

of operations. (Hint: Use Table 1 as a guide.) Since the project will be financed in part by debt, should the cash flow statement include interest expenses? Explain.

2. Should the $100 000 that was spent to rehabilitate the plant be included in the analysis? Explain.

3. Suppose another peach processor had expressed an interest in leasing the frozen peach dessert production site for $5000 a year. If this were true (in fact it was not), how would that information be incorporated into the analysis?

4. What is McReath's Year 0 net investment outlay on this project? What is the expected nonoperating cash flow when the project is terminated at Year 4? (Hint: Again, use Table 1 as a guide.)

5. Estimate the operating cash flows for Years 2, 3, and 4, and set forth the project's estimated net cash flow stream as a time line. What is the project's NPV, IRR, modified IRR (MIRR)[1], and payback? Should the project be undertaken? (Hint: The MIRR is found in three steps: (1) compound all net operating cash inflows forward to the terminal year at the cost of capital; (2) sum the compounded cash inflows to obtain the *terminal value* of the inflows; and (3) find the discount rate that forces the present value of the terminal value to equal the PV of the net investment outlays. This discount rate is defined as the MIRR.)

6. Now suppose the project had been a replacement rather than an expansion project. Describe briefly how the analysis would have to be changed to deal with a replacement project.

7. Assume that inflation is expected to average 5 percent per year over the next 4 years. Does it appear that the project's cash flow estimates are real or nominal? That is, are they stated in constant (current year) dollars, or has inflation been built into the cash flow estimates? Is the 10 percent cost of capital a nominal or a real rate? Is the current NPV biased, and, if so, in what direction?

8. a. Now assume that the sales price will increase by the 5 percent inflation rate beginning after Year 0. However, assume that cash operating costs will increase by only 2 percent annually from the initial cost estimate, because over half of the costs are fixed by long-term contracts. For simplicity, assume that no other cash flows (net externality costs, salvage value, or NWC) are affected by infla-

---

1 The MIRR is found in three steps: (1) compound all net operating cash inflows forward to the terminal year at the cost of capital; (2) sum the compounded cash inflows to obtain the *terminal value* of the inflows; and (3) find the discount rate that forces the present value of the terminal value to equal the PV of the net investment outlays. This discount rate is defined as the MIRR.

tion. What are the project's NPV, IRR, MIRR, and payback now that inflation has been taken into account? (Hint: The cash flow estimates are stated in Year 0 dollars, so both the Year 1 unit price and the Year 1 cash operating costs must be adjusted for inflation, along with succeeding years.)

b. What would happen to the project's profitability if inflation were neutral, that is, if both sales price and *cash costs* increased by the 5 percent annual inflation rate? Explain, but do not necessarily perform the calculations. If you are using the *Lotus* model, calculate the project's profitability in this situation and explain the results.

c. Now suppose that McReath is unable to pass along its inflationary input cost increases to its customers. For example, assume that cash costs increase by the 5 percent annual inflation rate, but that the sales price can be increased at only a 2 percent annual rate. Discuss the impact on the project's profitability. If you are using the *Lotus* model, complete the analysis.

9. Answer this question only if you are using the *Lotus* model. Return to the initial inflation assumptions (2 percent on price and 5 percent on cash costs).

a. Assume that the sales quantity estimate remains at 200 000 units per year. What Year 0 unit price would the company have to set to cause the project to just break even?

b. Now assume that the sales price remains at $2.00. What annual unit sales volume would be needed for the project to break even?

10. What assumption concerning the frozen peach dessert project's risk has been implicit in the analysis? Briefly explain how risk should be handled in capital budgeting. (Note that McReath Corporation (B) extends this case to include risk assessment and incorporation.)

11. The second capital budgeting decision that Joanne and Doug were asked to analyze involves choosing between two mutually exclusive projects, S and L, whose cash flows are set forth below:

Expected Net Cash Flow

Year	Project S	Project L
0	($100 000)	($100 000)
1	60 000	33 500
2	60 000	33 500
3	–	33 500
4	–	33 500

Both of these projects are in McReath's main line of business—peach juice—and the investment chosen is expected to be repeated indefinitely into the future. Also, each project is of average risk, and hence each is assigned the 10.0 percent corporate cost of capital.

a. What is each project's single-cycle NPV? Now apply the replacement chain approach, and then repeat the analysis using the equivalent annual annuity approach. Which project should be chosen, S or L?

b. Now assume that the cost to replicate Project S in 2 years is estimated to be $105 000 because of inflationary pressures. Similar investment cost increases will occur for both projects in the future. How would this affect the analysis? Which project should be chosen under this assumption?

12. The third project to be considered involves a fleet of trucks with an engineering life of 3 years (that is, the trucks will be totally worn out after 3 years). However, if the trucks were taken out of service, or "abandoned," prior to the end of 3 years, they would have a positive salvage value. Here are the estimated net cash flows for each truck:

Year	Initial Investment and Operating Cash Flow	End-of-Year Abandonment Cash Flow
0	($10 000)	$10 000
1	4 200	6 200
2	4 000	4 000
3	3 500	0

The relevant cost of capital is again 10 percent. What would the NPV be if the trucks were operated for the full 3 years? What if they were abandoned at the end of Year 2? At the end of Year 1? What is the economic life of the truck project?

Table 1
Selected Case Data

Net Investment Outlay

Price	X
Freight	X
Installation	X
Change in NWC	X
Net cost	X

Capital Cost Allowance Schedule

Year	CCA Rate	CCA	End-of-Year UCC
1	12.5%	$37 500	$262 500
2	25.0	X	196 875
3	25.0	X	X
4	25.0	X	X

Project Cash Flows

	Year 0	Year 1	Year 2	Year 3	Year 4
Unit price	$2 00	X	$2 00	X	$2 00
Unit sales		X	200 000	X	200 000
Revenues		X	$400 000	X	$400 000
Cash operating costs		X	300 000	X	300 000
Depreciation (CCA)		X	65 625	X	36 914
Net externality costs		X	10 000	X	10 000
Before-tax income		X	$ 24 375	X	$ 53 086
Taxes		X	9 750	X	21 234
Net income		X	$ 14 625	X	$ 31 852
Plus depreciation		X	65 625	X	36 914
Net operating cash flow		X	$ 80 250	X	$ 68 766
Salvage value					$110 742
Salvage value tax					X
Recovery of NWC					X
Termination cash flow					X
Project NCF	X	X	X	X	X

9

McReath Corporation (B)

In Case 8, McReath Corporation Part (A), Joanne Engel and Doug Bower analyzed a frozen peach dessert project for McReath Corporation. The project required an initial investment of $300 000 in fixed assets (including shipping and installation charges) plus a $10 000 addition to net working capital. The machinery would be used for 4 years and depreciated for tax purposes at a rate of 25% (12.5% in Year 1, and 25% in Years 2, 3, and 4). If the project is undertaken, the firm expects to sell 200 000 containers of the frozen peach dessert at a current dollar (Time 0) price of $2.00 a container. However, the sales price will be adjusted for inflation, which is expected to average 5 percent annually; so the expected sales price during the first year is $2.10, the expected price in the second year is $2.21, and so on.

Because the peach concentrate and the dessert are somewhat competitive, the frozen peach dessert project is expected to reduce the before-tax profit McReath currently earns on peach concentrate by $10 000. Further, the company expects cash operating costs to be $1.50 per unit in Time 0 dollars, and it expects these costs to increase by 2 percent per year. Therefore, total variable costs during Year 1 are expected to be ($1.50)(1.02)(200 000) = $306 000. McReath's tax rate is 40 percent, and its cost of capital is 10 percent. Selected cash flow data and other information as developed by Joanne and Doug, using a *Lotus 1-2-3* model, are given in Table 1.

When Joanne and Doug presented their analysis to McReath's executive committee, things went well, and the two were congratulated on both their analysis and their presentation. However, several questions were raised. In particular, the executive committee wanted to see some type of risk analysis on the project—it appeared to be profitable, but what were the chances that it might turn out to be a loser, and how should risk be analyzed and worked into the decision process? As the meeting was winding down, Joanne and Doug were asked to start with the base-case situation they had developed and then to discuss risk analysis, both in general terms and as it applies to the frozen peach dessert project.

To begin, Joanne and Doug met with the marketing and production managers to get a feel for the uncertainties involved in the cash flow estimates. After several sessions, they concluded that there was little uncertainty in any of the estimates except unit sales, which could vary widely. As estimated by the marketing staff, if product acceptance were normal, the sales quantity during Year 1 would be 200 000 units; if acceptance were poor, only 150 000 units would be sold (the price would remain at the forecasted level); while if consumer response were strong, this would produce a sales volume of 250 000 units for Year 1. In all cases, the price would increase at the 5 percent inflation rate: Hence, Year 1 revenues stated in Year 1 dollars, as it would appear on the income statement, would be $420 000 under the expected conditions, $315 000 if things went badly, and $525 000 if things went especially well. Cash costs per unit would remain at $1.50 before adjusting for inflation, so total cash costs in Year 1 would be approximately $306 000 under normal conditions, $230 000 in the worst-case scenario, and $383 000 in the best-case scenario. These costs would increase in each successive year at a 2 percent rate.

Joanne and Doug also talked about the scenarios' probabilities with the marketing staff. After considerable debate, they finally agreed on a "guesstimate" of a 25 percent probability of poor acceptance, a 50 percent probability of average (or base-case) acceptance, and a 25 percent probability of excellent acceptance.

Joanne and Doug also discussed with Hal Beerman, McReath's director of capital budgeting, both the risk inherent in McReath's average project and how the company typically adjusts for risk. Beerman told them that, based on historical data, McReath's average project has a coefficient of variation of NPV in the range of 0.25 to 0.50, and that the firm has been adding or subtracting 3 percentage points to its 10 percent overall cost of capital to adjust for differential project risk. When Joanne and Doug asked about the basis for the 3-percentage-point adjustment, Beerman stated that it apparently had no basis except the subjective judgement of Sy Smith, a former director of capital budgeting who was no longer with the company. Therefore, maybe the adjustment should be 2 percentage points, or maybe 5 percentage points or more.

The discussion with Beerman raised another issue: Should the project's cost of capital be based on its stand-alone risk, its risk as measured within the context of the firm's portfolio of assets, or in a market-risk context? McReath's target capital structure calls for 50 percent debt and 50 percent common equity, and the before-tax marginal cost of debt is estimated to be 11 percent. Joanne and Doug also estimated that the risk-free rate is 10 percent and that the market risk premium is 5 percent. They carefully considered the frozen peach dessert project's beta, and they finally agreed, based on some data from the Ontario Peach Growers Association, to use 1.5 as their best estimate of the beta for the equity invested in the project.

Since most members of McReath Corporation's executive committee are unfamiliar with modern techniques of financial analysis, the team was asked to again take a tutorial approach in their presentation. To structure their analysis, Joanne and Doug decided to ask and then answer the following questions.

Questions

1. **a.** Why should firms be concerned with the riskiness of individual projects?

   b. **(1)** What are the three levels, or types, of risk that are normally considered?

   (2) Which type of risk is most relevant for capital budgeting?

   (3) Which type of risk is easiest to measure?

   (4) Would you expect the three types of risk to generally be highly correlated? Would you expect them to be highly correlated in this specific instance?

2. **a.** What is sensitivity analysis?

   b. Replace the Xs in Table 1 and then develop a new table that shows a sensitivity analysis of NPV to sales quantity and the cost of capital. Assume that each of these variables can deviate from its base case, or expected value, by plus or minus 10%, 20%, and 30%. See Table 2 for partial results.

   c. Prepare a sensitivity diagram and discuss the results. See Figure 1 for a guide.

   d. If you are using the *Lotus* model, develop a table that shows the sensitivity of IRR to the same variables. Which variable has the greatest impact on IRR?

   e. What are the primary weaknesses of sensitivity analysis? What are its primary advantages?

3. **a.** What is the worst-case NPV? The best-case NPV?

   b. Use the worst-, most-likely-, and best-case NPVs, and their probabilities of occurrence, to find the project's expected NPV, standard deviation, and coefficient of variation. See Table 3 for a partially completed setup.

   c. What are the primary advantages and disadvantages of scenario analysis?

4. What is Monte Carlo simulation, and what are simulation's advantages and disadvantages vis-à-vis scenario analysis?

5. **a.** Would the frozen peach dessert project be classified as high risk, average risk, or low risk by your analysis thus far? What type of risk have you been measuring?

Figure 1
McReath Corporation
Sensitivity Analysis

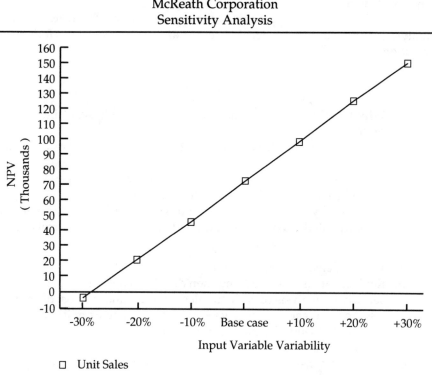

NPV (Thousands)

Input Variable Variability

□ Unit Sales

b. What do you think the project's within-firm risk would be, and how could you measure it?

c. How would it affect your risk assessment if you felt that the cash flows from this project were totally uncorrelated with McReath's other cash flows? What if they were negatively correlated?

d. How would the project's cash flows probably be correlated with the corporate profits of most other firms (say the TSE 300 Index), and hence with the stock market, and what difference would that make in the capital budgeting analysis?

6. Should the project be accepted? What if it had a CV of only 0.15 and was judged to be a low-risk project?

7. a. What is the project's market risk, and its required rate of return based on this risk? (Assume here that the risk-free rate is 10 percent, k_M = 15%, k_d = 11%, T = 40%, and the company's target capital structure calls for 50 percent debt.)

    b. Describe briefly two methods that might possibly be used to estimate the project's beta. Do you think those methods would be feasible in this case?

    c. What are the advantages and disadvantages of focusing on a project's market risk rather than on the other types of risk?

8. McReath Corporation is also evaluating two different systems for disposing of wastes associated with another product, peach yogurt. Plan W (for workers) requires more workers but less capital, while Plan C (for capital) requires more capital but fewer workers. Both systems have an estimated 3-year life, but the one selected will probably be repeated at the end of its life into the foreseeable future. Since the waste disposal choice has no impact on revenues, Joanne and Doug think that the decision should be based on the relative costs of the two systems; these costs are set forth next (in thousands of dollars). The Year 0 costs represent the capital outlays:

	Expected Net Costs	
Year	**Plan W**	**Plan C**
0	($500)	($1000)
1	(500)	(300)
2	(500)	(300)
3	(500)	(300)

    a. Assume initially that the two systems are both of average risk. Which one should be chosen?

    b. Now assume that the labour-intensive Plan W is judged to be riskier than an average project, because future labour costs are very difficult to forecast, but Plan C is still of average risk. McReath typically adds or subtracts 3 percentage points to its cost of capital when evaluating projects of differing risk. When these risk differences are considered, which system should be chosen?

9. During the presentation, Joanne and Doug were asked what the two waste disposal projects' IRRs and NPVs were. How would you answer that question?

Table 1
Selected Case Data

Net Investment Outlay

		CCA Schedule		

Net Investment Outlay

			CCA		
Price	$250 000				
Freight	20 000	Year	Rate	CCA	UCC
Installation	30 000				
Change in net		1	12.5%	$37 500	$262 500
working capital	10 000	2	25.0	65 625	196 875
	$310 000	3	25.0	X	X
		4	25.0	X	X

Project Cash Flows

	Year 0	Year 1	Year 2	Year 3	Year 4
Unit price	$2.00	$2 10	$2.21	X	$2.43
Unit sales		200 000	200 000	X	200 000
Revenues		$420 000	$441 000	X	$486 203
Cash operating costs		306 000	312 120	X	324 730
Depreciation (CCA)		37 500	65 625	X	36 914
Other project effects		10 000	10 000	X	10 000
Before-tax income		$ 66 500	$ 53 255	X	$114 559
Taxes		26 600	21 302	X	45 824
Net income		$ 39 900	$ 31 953	X	$ 68 735
Plus depreciation		37 500	65 625	X	36 914
Net operating cash flow		$ 77 400	$ 97 578	X	$105 649
Salvage value				X	$110 742
Recovery of NWC				X	10 000
Net terminal cash flow				X	$120 742
Projected net cash flow	($310 000)	$ 77 400	$ 97 578	X	$226 392

Decision Measures

NPV	X
IRR	X
MIRR	15.8%
Payback	3.2 years

Table 2
Sensitivity Analysis Results:
Frozen Peach Dessert Project

Variable Change from Base Level	Quantity	k
–30%	($ 6 103)	$102 316
–20	X	X
–10	45 394	81 125
0	71 142	71 142
10	X	X
20	122 639	52 306
30	148 388	43 415

Table 3
Scenario Analysis Results:
Frozen Peach Dessert Project

Case	Probability	NPV	IRR	MIRR
Worst	0.25	($ 6 771)	10.8%	10.6%
Most likely	0.50	71 142	18.5	15.8
Best	0.25	X	X	X
Expected value =		$71 142	18.4%	X
Standard deviation =		X	X	3.5%
Coefficient of variation =		X	0.3	0.2

10

Capital Budgeting
with Staged Entry

Computer-ese Incorporated

In July 1990, the senior executives of Computer-Ese Incorporated (CE), a leading computer manufacturer, scheduled a meeting to consider a significant change in corporate strategy. At present, CE's strategy is to concentrate on large mainframe computers that are connected to terminals throughout its customers' offices, rather than on smaller stand-alone computers. However, technological and marketing developments in the 1980s, including the rapid growth in the computing power and sales of personal computers, have prompted CE's management to reconsider the strategic plan. Management is now thinking of making a major move into the personal computer market.

CE was founded in 1972 by three former IBM computer engineers whose plan was to build top-of-the-line, large-scale computers. CE's products are regarded as being high quality, and the firm has the reputation of being a leader in its chosen line. However, it has never designed systems for either the small-business or the home markets. These two market segments were considered but rejected because (1) CE's technological and marketing advantages have always been in mainframes and (2) the company has never regarded the small-business and home markets as having the profit potential necessary to make the investment worthwhile. Recently, though, several competitors have entered the personal computer market, and there are signs that some of CE's large customers prefer to use stand-alone PCs for many of their applications rather than have everyone tied to the mainframe. Further, some mainframe components could be used in the PC line, and this could lead to economies of scale that could lower production costs.

CE's officers are examining a proposal for a two-stage, strategic move into personal computers. Stage 1 calls for the construction of a relatively unsophisticated, no-frills manufacturing plant with limited capacity. Stage 2 calls for the development of a major facility that would house the entire personal computer division—research and development, manufacturing, software development, marketing, and general management. CE originally considered developing a major facility at this time that would have required a much larger capital investment than Stage 1, and this facility would have had an operational life of at least 10 years. The main reason for the staged-entry plan, however, is that the Stage 2 expansion could be delayed or cancelled should things not work out well during Stage 1.

To date, CE has spent $7 million on research and development, including both design and marketing studies, on the new personal computer. Of this amount, $2 million have been expensed for tax purposes, while the remaining $5 million have been capitalized and will be amortized for tax purposes on a straight-line basis over the 5-year operating life of Stage 1. According to a Revenue Canada ruling specifically requested by CE, the capitalized R&D expenditures could be immediately expensed if the personal computer project is not undertaken.

If CE decides to build the plant, it would require a 20-acre site by December 31, 1990 ($t = 0$). The firm currently owns a suitable tract of land in an industrial park. The tract cost CE $500 000 several years ago, but it could be sold now for $1 million, net of realty fees and taxes. Other suitable sites could also be purchased for $1 million. The site currently owned was purchased by the Semiconductor Division, which plans an expansion in 1996. If the site is used for the personal computer production plant, CE would have to make other arrangements for the Semiconductor Division. CE can obtain an option on a similar site in the same park for a payment of $100 000 on December 31, 1990. The option would give CE the right to purchase the site on December 31, 1995 ($t = 5$) for a payment of $1.3 million. It is estimated that similar sites will then have a market value of $1.5 million, so the purchase could always be made at that time for the Semiconductor Division, should the currently owned tract be used for personal computers.

Most of 1991 would be spent obtaining provincial, county, and city approvals for the project, and the costs incurred would not be material to the decision. Plant construction would take place during 1992 at a cost of $8 million. For planning purposes, assume that the expenditure would occur on December 31, 1991 ($t = 1$). The building falls into Class 1 (Rate = 4%). Although its expected life is 30 years, the plant would actually be used for only 5 years, starting on January 1, 1994, with operating cash flows (end of year) occurring from December 31, 1994, through December 31, 1998 ($t = 4$ through $t = 8$). It is estimated that the land would have a market value of $2 million at the end of 1998, at which time the building would have a market value of $6 million.

The required production equipment would be obtained and installed during 1993 at a cost of $12 million (assume that payment would be made on December 31, 1992, or at $t = 2$). The equipment falls into Class 8 (Rate = 20%), and, as with the building, CCA would begin when operations commence, in 1994. At the end of 5 years, the wear and tear, along with technological obsolescence, would cause the equipment to be worth very little—the best estimate is only $1 million.

If CE builds the Stage 1 plant, the initial investment in net working capital would equal 30 percent of estimated first-year sales. (Assume that this investment would be made on December 31, 1993, at $t = 3$.) Additions to net working capital in each subsequent year would be 30 percent of the dollar sales increase expected in the following year. For example, any additional net working capital required to support the projected increase in 1995 sales over 1994 sales would be paid for on December 31, 1994.

CE's marketing department has projected sales of the personal computer at 25 000 units for 1993. Sales price is expected to be set at $3000. The production department has estimated manufacturing costs as follows:

> Variable costs: 65 percent of sales
> Fixed costs: $12 million annually, excluding depreciation.

Fixed costs, which include such things as managerial salaries and property taxes, but not depreciation, are expected to increase after 1994 at the expected rate of general inflation—4 percent. Unit sales are expected to increase at an annual rate of 10 percent as the product gains more and more market recognition and acceptance. The sales price, however, is expected to remain flat due to increasing competition in the personal computer market. Variable costs will remain at 65 percent of dollar sales, and hence will increase at the same rate as dollar sales, or 10 percent.

If the company decides to go forward with the project, Stage 2 would begin on December 31, 1996 ($t = 6$), when CE would have to spend $50.8 million on land and buildings. Capital investment would continue for two more years, and the operating cash flows (end of year) would begin the year following the shutdown of the Stage 1 plant. The Stage 2 net cash flows are forecasted as follows:

		Net Cash Flow	
End of Year	t	High Demand	Low Demand
1996	6	($ 50 800 000)	($50 800 000)
1997	7	(4 600 000)	(4 600 000)
1998	8	(1 600 000)	(1 600 000)
1999	9	20 000 000	17 000 000
2000	10	22 000 000	16 000 000
2001	11	24 000 000	15 000 000
2002	12	150 000 000	75 000 000

The net working capital from Stage 1 would be transferred to Stage 2 if it is undertaken. Stage 2 is projected to last beyond 2002, but cash flow estimation is so difficult when looking that far ahead that a terminal value, which incorporates the present value of cash flows beyond 2002, has been included in the 2002 cash flow.

CE's current federal-plus-provincial tax rate is 40 percent, and this rate is projected to remain fairly constant into the future. The firm's weighted average cost of capital is 11.0 percent, but CE adjusts this amount up or down by 2 percentage points for projects with substantially more or less risk than average.

Assume that you are the financial analyst charged with conducting the project analysis. Accordingly, it is your job to evaluate the project and to prepare a recommendation for CE's executive committee. In developing your recommendations, answer the following questions, which were posed by the financial vice-president, your boss.

Questions

1. Consider the land acquisition for Stage 1.
   a. What cost, if any, should be attributed to the personal computer project?
   b. Assuming that the currently owned site is used for this project, how should the Semiconductor Division obtain a site? What discount rate should be used in analyzing the option alternative?

2. Now think about the other cash flows associated with Stage 1.
   a. If Stage 1 is undertaken, what would the R&D cash flows be in 1994 through 1998? Should any R&D cash flow for 1990 be included in the Stage 1 analysis? Explain.
   b. Describe how salvage values are taxed. Use the building's salvage value to illustrate your answer.
   c. Complete the schedule of cash flows by filling in the blanks in Table 1.

3. Assume that the Stage 1 project is judged to be of average risk. What is its stand-alone NPV, IRR, MIRR, and payback?[1]

4. Now consider the expansion (Stage 2) project. What is its stand-alone NPV, IRR, and MIRR as of December 31, 1996 ($x = 6$) under each demand scenario? What are today's ($x = 0$) NPVs? What is Stage 2's expected NPV assuming there is a 70 percent probability that demand will be high during Stage 2, but a 30 percent chance that demand will be low? Again, assume that Stage 2 is an average-risk project.

5. CE estimates that there is an 80 percent chance that Stage 1 will meet all expectations, and consequently that Stage 2 will be undertaken. What is

---

1 The modified IRR (MIRR) is similar to the IRR except that the MIRR assumes reinvestment at the project's cost of capital, while the IRR assumes reinvestment at the IRR rate.

the expected NPV of CE's personal computer project? Using Figure 1 as a guide, construct a decision tree to help in the analysis.

6. Use the decision tree data to find the project's standard deviation and coefficient of variation of NPV. Suppose that CE's average project has a coefficient of variation of NPV in the range of 0.3 to 0.5. Would this project be classified as a high-, average-, or low-risk project?

7. What is the overall project's risk-adjusted NPV?

8. What do you think CE should do? Carefully justify your final conclusions.

9. Your boss, the financial vice-president, is concerned that the variable cost percentage used (65%) might be too low, and that variable costs might actually amount to 70 percent of dollar sales. If variable costs do amount to 70 or even 75 percent, how would this affect the NPV of Stage 1? If you are using the *Lotus* model, calculate the NPV at several higher variable cost percentages. Use an 11 percent cost of capital.

10. The marketing vice-president thinks the cash flow estimates for the Years 2000 to 2002 for the high-demand scenario of Stage 2 are inaccurate, so she asked you to use the following values:

Year	Cash Flow
2000	$ 21 000 000
2001	22 000 000
2002	100 000 000

She also asks you to assume that there is only a 60 percent chance that demand will be high during Stage 2 and a 40 percent chance that demand will be low. What would be the general effect of these changes on the expected NPV of the total computer project? Again, if you are using the *Lotus* model, what is the specific effect of these changes on NPV?

Figure 1
Personal Computer Project Decision Tree

		Joint	
	Stage 2: High Demand	NPV Probability	Product
Stage 1	Stage 2: Low Demand		
	Stop after Stage 1		
		Expected NPV =	

Table 1
Stage 1 Cash Flow Statements

End of Year	1990	1991	1992	1993	1994	1995	1996	1997	1998
Land	X								
R&D expense	X			X	X	X	X	X	X
Building		($8000)							
Equipment cost			($12 000)	X	X	X	X	X	X
Working capital				X	X	X	X	X	X
Total capital	X	($8000)	($12 000)	X	X	X	X	X	X
Sales					$75 000	$82 500	$90 750	$99 825	$109 808
Variable cost					48 750	53 625	58 988	64 886	71 375
Fixed cost					12 000	12 480	12 979	13 498	14 038
Depreciation					1 360	2 474	2 029	1 671	1 383
Operating income	$0	$ 0	$ 0	$0	$12 890	$13 921	$16 754	$19 769	$23 011
Tax	0	0	0	0	5 156	5 569	6 702	7 908	9 204
Net income	$0	$ 0	$ 0	$0	$ 7 734	$ 8 353	$10 053	$11 861	$ 13 807
Depreciation	0	0	0	0	1 360	2 474	2 029	1 671	1 383
Operating cash flow	$0	$ 0	$ 0	$0	$ 9 094	$10 826	$12 082	$13 533	$ 15 190
Land salvage value									X
Building salvage value									X
Equipment salvage value									X
Net cash flow	X	($8000)	($12 000)	$0	X	X	X	X	X

V

Dividend Policy

Case 11
Dividend Policy Northern Paper Company

11

Dividend Policy

Northern Paper Company

During the depression of the 1930s, Sidney Kaufman, a wealthy, expansion-oriented lumberman whose family had been in the forest products business in northern Ontario for several generations, began to acquire small, depressed paper companies. These businesses prospered during World War II, and, after the war, Kaufman anticipated that the demand for paper and lumber products would surge, so he aggressively sought new timberlands to supply his mills. In 1949, all of Kaufman's companies were consolidated, along with some other independent paper companies, into a single corporation, Northern Paper Company (NPC).

By 1990, NPC was a major force in the paper industry, though not one of the giants. Still, it possessed more timber and timberlands in relation to its use of timber than any other paper company. Worldwide demand for paper was strong, and its timber supply should have put Northern in a good position—with its assured supply of pulpwood, Northern could run its mills at a steady rate and thus at a low per-unit production cost. However, the company does not have sufficient manufacturing capacity to fully utilize its timber supplies, so it has been forced to sell wood to other paper companies to generate cash flow, and to give up potential profits in the process.

NPC has enjoyed rapid growth in both sales and assets. This rapid growth has, however, caused some financial problems, as indicated in Table 1. The condensed balance sheets shown in the table reveal that NPC's financial leverage has increased substantially in the last 20 years, while the firm's liquidity position markedly deteriorated over the same period. Remember, though, that the balance sheet figures reflect *historical* costs, and that the market values of the assets could be much higher than the values shown on the balance sheet. For example, Northern purchased 10 000 acres of cut timberland in 1959 for $10 per acre, then planted trees that are now mature. The value of this acreage and its timber is estimated at $2750 per acre, even though it is shown on the firm's balance sheet at $230 per acre, the

Table 1
Northern Paper Company
Condensed Balance Sheets
Years Ended December 31
(Millions of Dollars)

	1970	1980	1990
Cash and marketable securities	$ 18.0	$ 30.0	$ 16.0
Accounts receivable	35.0	67.3	178.4
Inventories	22.5	27.9	70.6
Total current assets	$ 75.5	$125.2	$ 265.0
Fixed assests (net)	68.2	241.5	813.4
Total assets	$143.7	$366.7	$1078.4
Current liabilities	$ 17.2	$ 43.3	$ 177.8
Long-term debt	31.0	122.0	404.0
Common equity	95.5	201.4	496.6
Total liabilities and net worth	$143.7	$366.7	$1078.4
Current ratio (2.5×)[a]	4.4×	2.9×	1.5×
Ratio of cash and marketable securities to current liabilities (.5×)[a]	1.0×	0.7×	0.09×
Debt ratio (30%)[a]	34%	45%	54%

[a] The numbers in parentheses represent industry averages, which were relatively stable over the 20-year period.

original $10 plus capitalized planting costs. Note also that this particular asset and others like it have produced zero accounting income; indeed, expenses associated with this acreage have produced accounting losses.

When NPC was originally organized, most of the outstanding stock was owned by Kaufman and by members of his family. Over time, however, Kaufman's ownership position has gradually declined due to the issuance of new common stock to fund the expansion program. By the end of 1990, Kaufman and his family held only about 35 percent of NPC's common stock, and this represented essentially their entire net worth.

Kaufman has sought to finance the firm's growth with internally generated funds to the greatest extent possible. Hence, NPC has never declared a cash dividend, nor has it had a stock dividend or a stock split. Due to the plowback of earnings, the stock currently sells for almost $2000 per share. Kaufman has stated a strong belief that investors prefer low-payout stocks because of their tax advantages, and he also thinks that stock dividends and stock splits serve no useful purpose—according to him, they merely create more pieces of paper but no incremental value for shareholders. Finally, Kaufman feels that higher-priced stocks are more attractive to investors because the percentage of brokerage commissions on small purchases of higher-priced stocks is lower than on large purchases of lower-priced shares. He cites the example of Graham-Cheney, whose stock price has risen phenomenally, even though it sells for over $6000 per share and pays no dividends. (Kaufman does acknowledge, though, that Warren Melnick, Graham-Cheney's chairman, has done a superb job of managing the company's assets, and that the rise of its stock reflects that factor as well as Melnick's financial policies.)

As the date for NPC's annual stockholders' meeting approached, Peter Cohen, the corporate secretary, informed Kaufman that an unusually low number of shareholders had sent in their proxies. Cohen felt that this might be due to rising discontent over the firm's dividend policy. During the last ten years, the average payout for firms in the paper industry has been between 30 and 40 percent, yet for the fortieth straight year, NPC's board, under Kaufman's dominance, chose not to pay a dividend in 1989. Kaufman was also aware that several reports in the financial press in recent months indicated that NPC was a possible target of a takeover attempt. Since he did not want to lose control of the company, Kaufman was anxious to keep the firm's stockholders as happy as possible. Accordingly, he announced that the directors would hold a special meeting immediately after the annual meeting to consider whether the firm's dividend policy should be changed.

Kaufman instructed Dana Harrison, NPC's financial vice-president, to identify and then evaluate alternative dividend policies in preparation for the special board meeting. He asked her to consider both cash dividends, stock dividends, and stock splits. Harrison then identified six alternatives that she thought deserved further consideration:

(1)   **No cash dividends, no stock dividend or split.** This was the position that Harrison was certain Kaufman would support, both for the reasons given above and also because he thought the company, as evidenced by the balance sheet, was in no position to pay cash dividends.

(2)   **Immediate cash dividend, but no stock dividend or split.** This was simply the opposite of the no-dividend policy. If a cash dividend policy were instituted, its size would still be an issue.

(3)   **Immediate cash dividend plus a large stock split.** The stock split would be designed to lower the price of the firm's stock from its current price of almost $2000 per share to somewhere in the average price range of other large paper stocks, or from $20 to $40 per share.

(4)   **Immediate cash dividend plus a large stock dividend.** The reasoning underlying this policy would be essentially the same as that of Alternative 3.

(5)   **Cash dividend, stock split, and periodic stock dividends.** This policy would require the company to declare an immediate cash dividend and, simultaneously, to announce a sizeable stock split. This policy would go farther than Alternatives 3 and 4 in that after the cash dividend and stock split or large stock dividend, the company would

Table 2
Northern Paper Company
Selected Information

	Northern Paper Company			Industry Averages	
Year	Earnings per Share	Book Value per Share	Average Market Price per Share	P/E Ratio	M/B Ratio
1970	$ 68	$ 560	$ 680	10×	1.2×
1975	100	824	1253	17×	2.5×
1980	106	1180	1360	18×	2.6×
1985	109	1769	1597	19×	2.9×
1990	143	2483	1902	16×	2.5×

Period	Industry Average Annual Compound Growth Rate in Earnings per Share
1970–1975	7%
1975–1980	6
1980–1985	7
1985–1990	8

periodically declare smaller stock dividends equal in value to the earnings retained during the period. In effect, if the firm earned $3 per share in any given period—quarter, semiannual period, and so on—and retained $1.50 per share, the company would also declare a stock dividend of a percentage amount equal to $1.50 divided by the market price of the stock. Thus, if the firm's shares were selling for $30 when the cash dividend was paid, a 5 percent stock dividend would be declared.

(6) Share repurchase plan. This plan is based on the premise that investors in the aggregate would like to see the company distribute some cash, but that some stockholders would not want to receive cash dividends because they want to minimize their taxes. Under the repurchase plan, individual stockholders could decide for themselves whether or not to sell some or all of their shares and thus to realize some cash and some capital gains, depending on their own situations.

To begin her evaluation, Dana Harrison collected the data shown in Table 2. As she was looking over these figures, Harrison wondered what effect, if any, NPC's dividend policy had on the company's stock price as compared with the prices of other stocks. Harrison is also aware of one other issue—one that neither she nor anyone else has had the nerve to bring up. Kaufman is 79 years old, he is not in the best of health, and in recent years he has been almost obsessed with the idea of avoiding taxes. Further, the federal and provincial tax rate is currently near 60 percent, and additional probate fees would be due, so well over half of Kaufman's net worth as of the date of his death may have to be paid out in income and probate taxes. Since capital gains and probate taxes are based on the value of the assets on the date of death, to minimize these taxes, Kaufman might not want the value of the company to be maximized until after his death. Harrison does not know Kaufman's view of this, but she does know that his tax advisers have thought it through and have explained it to him.

Finally, Harrison knows that several Bay Street firms have been analyzing Northern's "breakup value," or the value of the company if it were broken up and sold off in pieces. She has heard breakup value estimates as high as $3500 per share, primarily because other paper companies, including Japanese and European companies, are eager to buy prime properties such as those of NPC. Of course, NPC could sell assets on its own, but Harrison does not expect that to happen as long as Kaufman is in control.

Now assume that you are Dana Harrison's assistant, and that she has asked you to help her with the analysis by answering the following questions and then discussing your answers with her and Kaufman. Kaufman is famous for asking tough questions and then crucifying the person being questioned if he or she has trouble responding, and that is probably why Harrison wants you to make the presentation. So, be sure that you thoroughly understand the questions and your answers, and that you can handle any follow-up questions that you might get.

Questions

1. For each of the years listed in Table 2, what are NPC's P/E ratio and market/book ratio? What are the firm's earnings per share growth rates for the intervals listed in Table 2? Compare your answers with the industry averages shown in Table 2. What can be inferred about NPC's dividend policy from these data?

2. Do you think it is better for firms in general, and for NPC in particular, to have an announced dividend policy?

3. In general, how is a firm's growth rate in earnings per share affected by its dividend policy? What does this imply about NPC's historical rate of return on investment vis-à-vis that of the average paper company? (Hint: Consider the retention growth model, $g = br$, where g = growth rate in EPS, b = retention ratio, and r = return on equity.)

4. Evaluate Kaufman's argument that higher-priced stocks are more attractive to investors because the percentage transactions costs on such issues are lower. Is this a valid argument? Do you think NPC's current per-

share price is "optimal" in the sense that the value of the shares to investors is maximized? Explain.

5. In general, and in this case, what impact should a firm's use of financial leverage have on its dividend policy?

6. Evaluate the alternative dividend policies that have been proposed. Discuss the implications of each of these positions for NPC.

7. Considering NPC's present financial condition, do you think the company is a likely target for a hostile takeover attempt? What effect would the firm's dividend policy have on its vulnerability to a takeover? How might the company use a restructuring that involved asset sales to reduce the threat of a takeover?

8. How should you deal with Kaufman's tax situation? Should you bring it up, and if so, in what context and with what recommendation? If Kaufman does indeed want to hold down the price of the stock (but not hurt the long-run value of the corporation), should the other directors go along with him? How would "the market" be likely to deal with the situation, assuming that they have no information whatever regarding what is said or not said about it within the company?

9. What stockholder clientele do you believe currently owns most of NPC's stock? What impact does stockholder composition have on a firm's dividend policy?

10. What dividend policy do you think NPC should follow? First, should NPC declare a stock split and/or a stock dividend, and if so, how large should it be? Second, should any assets be sold, and if so, should the proceeds be used to pay dividends, to retire debt, to build new plants, or for some other purpose? Finally, if you think cash dividends should be paid, how large should the initial payment be, what dividend growth rate should be targeted, and should the change in policy be announced? Explain your answers, and if you do not think you have enough information to give a precise quantitative answer to any part of the question, explain how you would go about developing a quantitative answer if you had access to all the company's data and internal information.

VI

Long-Term Financing Decisions

Case 12
Going Public Capital City Savings and Loan

Case 13
Bond Refunding East Coast Electric

Case 14
Lease Analysis Bunbury Chemical Company

Case 15
Financing with Convertibles and Warrants Weaver Foods, Inc.

12

Capital City Savings and Loan

Capital City Savings and Loan was founded in 1964 in Victoria, British Columbia, which is just across the Georgia Strait from Vancouver. Victoria is very popular with visitors to British Columbia, and also a popular place for many Canadians to spend their retirement years. Per capita income in Victoria is substantially above the national average. The combination of an increasing population, high per capita income, and a huge demand for funds to finance new home construction has made Capital City the fastest-growing association in the province in terms of both assets and earnings.

Although Capital City is very profitable and its earnings have been increasing at a rapid pace, the company's quick expansion has put it under severe financial strain. Even though all earnings have been retained, the equity-to-assets ratio has been declining to the extent that, by 1990, it was just above the minimum required regulation (see Table 1).

Capital City now has the opportunity to open a branch office in a new shopping centre. If the office is opened, it will bring in profitable new loans and deposits, further increasing the association's growth. However, an inflow of deposits at the present time would cause the equity-to-assets ratio to fall below the minimum requirement. Consequently, Capital City must raise additional equity funds of approximately $3 million if it is to open the new branch.

Even though Capital City has a ten-member board of directors, the company is completely dominated by the three founders and major stock-holders: Bob McRae, chairman of the board and owner of 35 percent of the stock; Richard Harris, president and owner of 35 percent of the stock; and John Brandt, a builder serving as a director of the company and owner of 20 percent of the stock. The remaining 10 percent of the stock is owned by the other seven directors. McRae and Brandt both have substantial outside financial interests. Most of Harris's net worth is represented by his stock in Capital City.

Table 1
Capital City Savings and Loan
Balance Sheet for Year Ended December 31, 1990

Assets[a]		
Cash and marketable securities	$ 83 441 700	
Mortgage loans	815 235 000	
Fixed assets	60 423 300	
Total assets		$959 100 000
Liabilities		
Savings accounts	$817 153 200	
Other liabilities	83 077 000	
Capital stock ($100 par value)	900 000	
Retained earnings	57 969 800	
Total claims		$959 100 000

[a] Regulations require the ratio of capital plus retained earnings-to-assets to be at least 6 percent.

McRae, Harris, and Brandt agree that Capital City should obtain the additional equity funds to make the branch expansion possible. They are not in complete agreement, however, as to how the additional funds should be raised. They could raise the additional capital by having Capital City sell newly issued shares to a few of their friends and associates. The other alternative is to sell shares to the general public. The three men themselves cannot put additional funds into the company at the present time.

McRae favours the private sale. He points out that he, Harris, and Brandt have all been receiving substantial amounts of ancillary, or indirect, income from the savings and loan operation. The three men jointly own a holding company that operates an insurance agency that writes insurance for many of the homes financed by Capital City; they jointly own a title insurance corporation that deals with the association; and Brandt owns a construction company that obtains loans from the association. McRae maintains that these arrangements could be continued without serious problems if the new capital were raised by selling shares to a few individuals, but questions of conflict of interest would probably arise if the stock were sold to the general public. He also opposes a public offering on the grounds that the flotation cost would be high for a public sale, but would be virtually zero if the new stock were sold to a few individual investors.

Harris disagrees with McRae. He feels that it would be preferable to sell the stock to the general public rather than to a limited number of investors. Acknowledging that flotation costs on the public offering are a consideration, and that conflict-of-interest problems may occur if shares of the company are sold to the general public, he argues that there would be several offsetting advantages if the stock were publicly traded: (1) the existence of a market-determined price would make it easier for the present stockholders to

Table 2
Capital City Savings and Loan
Selected Information

Year	Net Profit	Earnings per Share
1990	$8 562 780	$951.42
1989	7 476 390	830.71
1988	6 521 490	724.61
1987	5 231 610	581.29
1986	4 712 220	523.58
1985	3 905 550	433.95

borrow money, using their shares in Capital City as collateral for loans; (2) the existence of a public market would make it possible for current shareholders to sell some of their shares on the market if they needed cash for any reason; (3) having the stock publicly traded would make executive stock option plans more attractive to key employees of the company; (4) establishing a market price for the shares would simplify problems of valuation in the event of the death of one of the current stockholders; and (5) selling stock to the public now would facilitate acquiring additional equity capital in the future.

Brandt, whose 20 percent ownership of the company gives him the power to cast the deciding vote, is unsure whether he should back the public sale or the private offering. He thinks that additional information is needed to help clarify the issues.

The board therefore instructed Patricia Rizutto, Capital City's chief financial officer, to study the issue and to report back in two weeks. As a first

Table 3
Data on Publicly Traded
Savings and Loan Associations

	Assets (Millions)	Equity (Millions)	Book Value per Share	Stock Price	EPS 1990	EPS 1985
BC Financial Capital, Inc.	$14 000	$ 950	$30.30	$32.00	$5.25	$2.50
First Financial, Inc.	30 500	2020	16.15	17.00	2.00	0.83
The Great North Capital Corp.	24 000	1130	38.95	25.00	5.40	1.59
Western Financial Corp.	27 000	1400	56.50	28.00	6.25	3.94

step, Rizutto obtained the data on Capital City's earnings given in Table 2. Rizutto then collected information on four publicly traded savings and loan associations; these data are shown in Table 3. She then set about the task of coming up with a recommendation for the board of directors. Unfortunately, Rizutto had prior plans to attend an out-of-town meeting, and hence she drafted a set of questions for you, her assistant, to answer. She will meet with you on her return to discuss your findings. Knowing Rizutto's passion for detail, you plan to fully explain your answers.

Questions

1. Using information contained in Table 1, calculate Capital City's equity-to-assets ratio, the number of shares of stock outstanding, and the book value per share of common stock for 1990.

2. Using the data in Table 2, calculate Capital City's average annual growth rate in earnings per share from 1985 to 1990. (Hint: In your calculations, use only the data for 1985 and 1990.)

3. For the four companies listed in Table 3, calculate the following:
   a. The equity-to-assets ratios for 1990.
   b. Average annual growth rates in earnings per share for the 5-year period from 1985 through 1990.
   c. The price/earnings ratios in 1990.
   d. The market-value-to-book-value ratios for 1990.

4. Considering your answers to Questions 1 through 3, develop a range of values that you think would be reasonable for Capital City's market-to-book ratio if it were a publicly held company.

5. Regardless of your answer to Question 4, assume that 0.8× is an appropriate market-value-to-book-value ratio for Capital City. What would be the market value per share of the company?

6. Investment dealers generally like to offer the initial stock of companies that are going public at a price ranging from $10 to $30 per share. If Capital City stock were to be offered to the public at a price of $20 per share, how large a stock split would be required prior to the sale?

7. Assume that Capital City chooses to raise $3 million through the sale of stock to the public at $20 per share.
   a. Approximately how large would the percentage flotation cost be for such an issue?
   b. How many shares of stock would have to be sold in order for Capital City to pay the flotation cost and receive $3 million net proceeds from the offering?

8. Assume that each of the three major stockholders decided to sell half of his stock.
   a. How many shares of stock and what total amount of money (assuming that the stock split occurred and that these shares were sold at a price of $20 per share) would be involved in this secondary offering? (A secondary offering is defined as the sale of stock that is already issued and outstanding. The proceeds of such offerings accrue to the individual owners of the stock, not to the company.)
   b. Approximately what percentage flotation cost would be involved if the investment dealers were to combine the major stockholders' secondary offering with the sale by the company of sufficient stock to provide it with $3 million?

9. Can you see why McRae and Harris might have personal reasons for their differences of opinion on the question of public ownership? Explain.

10. The analysis was based on the comparability of Capital City with four other savings institutions. What factors might tend to invalidate the comparison?

11. All things considered, do you feel that Capital City should go public? Fully justify your conclusion.

13

Bond Refunding

East Coast Electric

Rod Beecham, financial vice-president of East Coast Electric, has just begun reviewing the minutes of the company's last board of directors meeting. The major topic discussed at the meeting was whether East Coast should refund any of its currently outstanding bond issues. Of particular interest is a $400 million, 30-year, 12 percent, first-mortgage bond issued approximately 5 years ago. Four of the board members had taken markedly different positions on the question, and at the conclusion of the meeting, Ted MacDonald, chairman of the board, asked Beecham to prepare a report analyzing the alternative points of view.

The bonds in question had been issued in January 1986, when interest rates were relatively high. It was necessary to issue the bonds at that time, despite the high interest rates, because East Coast needed to complete an additional coal-fired plant immediately if it was to meet future demand for electricity in the area it served. At that time, Beecham and the board strongly believed interest rates were at a peak and would decline in the future, but they were unsure of when rates would fall or by how much. Now, almost 5 years later, with lower rates, East Coast can sell A-rated bonds that yield significantly less than 12 percent.

Since Beecham had anticipated a decline in interest rates when he sold the $400 million issue, he had insisted that the bonds be made callable after 5 years. (If the bonds had not been callable, East Coast would have had to pay an interest rate of only 11 percent, a full percentage point less than the actual 12 percent.) The bonds can be called after January 1, 1991, but a call premium of 10 percent, or $100 per bond, would have to be paid. This premium declines by 12%/30 = 0.4 percentage points, or $4.00, each year. Thus, if the bonds were called in 1996, the call premium would be (0.12/30)(20) = 8.0 percent, or $80, where 20 represents the number of years remaining to maturity. The flotation costs on this issue amounted to one percent of the issue, or $4 million.

Beecham estimates that East Coast can sell a new issue of 25-year bonds at an interest rate of 10 percent. The call of the old and sale of the new bonds could take place 5 to 7 weeks after the decision to refund has been made; this time is required to give legal notice to bondholders and to arrange the $400 million or more needed to pay them off. The flotation cost on the refunding issue would also be 1 percent of the new issue's face amount, and funds from the new issue would be available from the underwriters the day they were needed to pay off the old bonds.

Beecham had proposed at the last directors meeting that the company call the 12 percent bonds and refund them with a new 10 percent issue. (The bonds could not have been called earlier because of the call protection provision in the indenture.) Although the refunding cost would be substantial, he believed the interest savings of 2 percent per year for 25 years on a $400 million issue would be well worth the cost. Beecham did not anticipate adverse reactions from the other board members; however, four of them voiced strong doubts about the refunding proposal. The first was John Ritchie, a long-term member of East Coast's board and chairman of Ritchie, Mooney & Company, an investment company catering primarily to institutional clients such as insurance companies and pension funds. Ritchie argued that calling the bonds for refunding would not be well received by the major financial institutions that hold the firm's outstanding bonds. According to Ritchie, the institutional investors who hold the bonds had purchased them on the expectation of receiving the 12 percent interest rate for at least 10 years, and these investors would be very disturbed by a call after only 5 years. Since most of the leading institutions hold some of East Coast's bonds, and since the firm typically sells new bonds or common stock to finance its growth every 2 or 3 years, it would be most unfortunate if institutional investors developed a feeling of ill will toward the company.

A second director, Sean O'Donnell, who was a relatively new member of the board and vice-president of the Eastern Region of the National Bank of Canada, also opposed the call, but for an entirely different reason. O'Donnell believed that the decline in interest rates was not yet over. He said a study by his bank suggested that the long-term interest rate might fall to as low as 8 percent within the next 6 months. Under questioning from the other board members, however, O'Donnell admitted that the interest rate decline could in fact be over and that interest rates might, very shortly, begin to move back up again. When pressed, O'Donnell produced the following probability distribution that his economists had developed for interest rates on A-rated utility issues one year from now, on January 1, 1992:

Probability	Interest Rate on A-rated Utility Issues
0.1	8.0%
0.2	9.5
0.4	10.5
0.2	11.5
0.1	13.0

The third director, Pierre Gosselin, requested more information on the refunding. Gosselin suggested that a formal analysis using discounted cash flow (DCF) techniques be employed to determine the profitability of the refunding. As he reflected on Gosselin's proposal, Beecham wondered whether it might be better to modify the DCF analysis, if it were used, by employing East Coast's cost of debt rather than its average cost of capital. Further, if the cost of debt were used, he wondered whether a before- or after-tax figure should be employed.

The fourth director, Anne McGillivray, East Coast's treasurer, stated that she was not against the refunding, but wondered whether it was wise to sell the new bonds and call the old bonds at essentially the same time. McGillivray was worried that something might go wrong, keeping East Coast from obtaining the cash generated by the sale of the new bonds in time to pay for the repurchase of the old bonds. Therefore, McGillivray suggested that East Coast issue the new bonds 2 to 3 weeks before the refunding of the old bonds to ensure that sufficient cash is on hand when the old bonds are repurchased. McGillivray also noted that the funds generated by the sale of the new bonds could be invested in treasury securities yielding 7 percent during this overlap period. Finally, she noted that interest rates had been quite volatile lately, and that if rates rose before the new issue could be sold, the refunding would be a disaster. Therefore, McGillivray wondered if East Coast could "lock in a profit" and thus protect itself against rising interest rates by assuming a position in the futures market.

As Beecham's assistant, you have been asked to draft responses to the following questions.

Questions

1. What discount rate should be used to perform the refunding analysis? Discuss the relative merits of using the current after-tax bond rate as opposed to the after-tax average cost of capital. (Hint: Think about the probability distributions of cash flows from the refunding operation versus cash flows from a "typical" project.)

2. Calculate the net present value of the refunding if East Coast goes ahead with the new bond issue on January 1, 1991. Assume that the firm has a 40 percent marginal tax rate. Use Table 1 as a guide for your analysis. (Note: Canadian tax treatment of the flotation cost is to amortize the amount on a straight-line basis over 5 years.)

3. Give a critique of each of the positions taken by the various board members. As a part of your answer, calculate the expected NPV of refunding next year based on O'Donnell's probability distribution of interest rates. Remember, however, that if East Coast refunds next year, the old bonds will have 24 years left to maturity. Assume for purposes

of this question that East Coast could issue the new bonds with a 24-year maturity. Also, remember that East Coast would not act next year if the refunding had a negative NPV at that time.

4. Should the refunding operation be undertaken at this time?

5. How would the nature of the probability distribution of expected future interest rates affect the decision to refund now or to wait? Draw two probability distribution curves on the same chart, with one curve suggesting that the refunding be deferred, and with the other suggesting that the refunding take place immediately. (Hint: There is no single correct answer. Think about the expected values and shapes of the distributions.)

6. Suppose the major bond-rating agencies downgraded East Coast's credit rating from A to B^{++} before East Coast could initiate the refunding, such that selected data given in the case changed as follows:
   (1) The coupon rate on the new bond is 11.2 percent.
   (2) The flotation cost on the new bonds is 1.5 percent of the issue's face value, or $6 million.
   How would these factors affect the refunding decision?

7. If the yield curve had been downward sloping, and if Beecham felt that "the market knows more than I do" about the future course of interest rates, how might this affect his decision to recommend immediate refunding versus deferring the refunding?

8. How would East Coast's position as a regulated public utility affect the accept/reject decision on the bond refunding? Would East Coast have more or less incentive to refund than an unregulated company? (Hint: Regulators set rates so that utilities just earn their costs of capital.)

9. Another bond that East Coast is considering refunding is a $200 million, 30-year issue sold 25 years ago in January 1966. At the time this bond was issued, East Coast was in poor financial condition and was considered to be a high credit risk. To raise the $200 million, East Coast was forced to issue subordinated debentures with a B$^+$ rating and a coupon rate of 10.6 percent (the call premium is now 1% on this issue), which was quite high at the time. The flotation cost on this issue was 1.5 percent of the face amount, or $3 million. Rod Beecham estimates that East Coast could also refund this $200 million issue with a 25-year, 10 percent coupon bond that would require a flotation cost of $2 million. Assume that this $200 million of capital will be needed into the indefinite future, so whether the bond is refunded now or in 5 years, it will subsequently be refunded every 25 years with a 25-year, 10 percent bond, with each successive replacement bond remaining outstanding to its maturity. Is the refunding analysis you used in Question 2 appropriate for this bond? Explain how the analysis could be modified to make it better, and if you

are using the *Lotus* model, complete the numerical analysis. (Hint: Use Table 2 as a guide.)

10. Describe how East Coast could use the futures market to protect against a possible interest rate increase between the time the decision is made to refund the old issue and the time the refunding actually takes place. If you are using the *Lotus* model, calculate how much interest rates can increase before the refunding becomes unprofitable.

11. Do you think that a lower tax rate, say 20 percent, would make the refunding more or less attractive? If you are using the *Lotus* model, show the relationship between refunding NPV and tax rate.

12. If you are using the *Lotus* model, run the refunding analyses at a range of interest rates, and then create a graph showing the relationship between the refunding interest rate and NPV.

Table 1
Bond Refunding Analysis

	Amount Before Tax	Amount After Tax	Present Value
Cost of Refunding at t = 0			
Call premium on old issue	($40 000 000)	($40 000 000)	($40 000 000)
Flotation cost on new issue	X	X	X
Tax savings on old floatation expense	0	0	0
Net investment outlay			X
Flotation Cost Tax Effect			
New issue tax amortization	$ 800 000	$ 320 000	X
Old issue amortization	0	0	0
Net present value of flotation cost effect			$ 1 347 956
Interest Savings Due to Refunding			
Annual payment (old bond)	$48 000 000	$28 800 000	
Annual payment (new bond)	40 000 000	X	
Net annual savings and present value		X	X
NPV of the refunding decision			X

Table 2
Replacement Chain Analysis

	After-Tax Cash Flow (Interest Expense + Flotation Cost)	
Year	Delay Refund	Refund Now
0	0	(4 000 000)*
1	(12 680 000)	(11 968 000)
2	X	X
3	(12 680 000)	(11 968 000)
4	(12 680 000)	(11 968 000)
5	(14 680 000)*	(11 968 000)
6	(11 968 000)	(11 968 000)
7	(11 968 000)	(11 968 000)
8	(11 968 000)	(11 968 000)
9	(11 968 000)	(11 968 000)
10	(11 968 000)	(11 968 000)
11	(11 968 000)	(11 968 000)
12	(11 968 000)	(11 968 000)
13	(11 968 000)	(11 968 000)
14	(11 968 000)	(11 968 000)
15	(11 968 000)	(11 968 000)
16	(11 968 000)	(11 968 000)
17	(11 968 000)	(11 968 000)
18	(11 968 000)	(11 968 000)
19	(11 968 000)	(11 968 000)
20	(11 968 000)	(11 968 000)
21	(11 968 000)	(11 968 000)
22	(11 968 000)	(11 968 000)
23	(11 968 000)	(11 968 000)
24	(11 968 000)	(11 968 000)
25	(11 968 000)	X*
26	(11 968 000)	(11 968 000)
27	(11 968 000)	(11 968 000)
28	(11 968 000)	(11 968 000)
29	(11 968 000)	(11 968 000)
30	X*	(11 968 000)
31	(11 968 000)	(11 968 000)
32	(11 968 000)	(11 968 000)
⋮	⋮	⋮

* indicates a refunding year.

14

Lease Analysis

Bunbury Chemical Company

Over the past few years, officials in Alberta and other locations that rely primarily on deep groundwater for drinking water have become aware of a potentially serious problem—the pollution of aquifers by the unrestrained use of fertilizers and pesticides. The results of a study conducted by the Canadian Geological Survey showed that while the main water aquifer underlying the province is not yet contaminated, one chemical commonly found in agricultural pesticides has caused extensive contamination of wells that tap water-bearing strata near the surface. To combat this potentially widespread problem, officials in Alberta and elsewhere are lobbying for strict environmental regulation of fertilizers and pesticides that do not adhere to newly proposed safety standards. As a result, companies specializing in agricultural chemicals have been working furiously to supply new products that will not be banned under the proposed regulations.

Bunbury Chemical Company, a regional producer of agricultural chemicals, recently developed a pesticide that meets the new regulations. Now the firm must acquire the necessary equipment to begin production. The estimated internal rate of return (IRR) of this project is 24 percent, and the project was judged to have low risk. Bunbury uses an after-tax cost of capital of 11 percent for relatively low-risk projects, 13 percent for those of average risk, and 15 percent for high-risk projects, so this low-risk project passed with flying colours.

The equipment has an invoice price of $300 000, including delivery and installation charges, and is a Class 10 asset (Capital Cost Allowance [CCA] Rate = 30%). Bunbury's effective tax rate is 40 percent. The manufacturer of the equipment will provide a contract for maintenance and service for $15 000 per year, payable at the beginning of each year, if Bunbury decides to buy the equipment.

Regardless of whether the equipment is purchased or leased, Joan Haddad, the firm's financial manager, does not think that it will be used for more than 4 years, at which time Bunbury's current building lease will expire. Land on which to construct a larger facility has already been acquired, and the building should be ready for occupancy at that time. The new facility will be designed to enable Bunbury to use several new production processes that are currently unavailable to it, including one that will duplicate all processes of the equipment now being considered. Hence, the current project is viewed as a "bridge" to serve only until the permanent equipment can become operational in the new facility 4 years from now. The expected useful life of the equipment is 8 years, at which time it should have a zero market value, but the residual value at the end of the fourth year should be well above zero. Haddad generally assumes that assets' salvage values will be equal to their Undepreciated Capital Cost (UCC) at any point in time, but she is concerned about that assumption in this instance.

Currently, the company has sufficient capital in the form of temporary investments in marketable securities to pay cash for the equipment and the first year's maintenance. Haddad estimates that the interest rate on a 4-year secured loan for $300 000 would be 10 percent, but she has decided to draw down the securities portfolio and pay cash for the equipment if it is purchased.

Western Capital, Inc., a major leasing company, has offered to lease the equipment to Bunbury for annual payments of $85 000, with the first payment due upon delivery and installation and additional payments due at the beginning of each succeeding year of the 4-year lease term. This price includes a service contract under which the equipment would be maintained in good working order. Western Capital would buy the equipment from the manufacturer under the same terms that were offered to Bunbury, including the maintenance and service contract. Like Bunbury, Western Capital generally assumes that the most likely residual value for equipment of this type is the UCC at the end of the lease term. Some Western Capital executives, however, think that the residual value in this case will be much higher because of the expanding nature of the business. Western Capital is not expected to pay any taxes over the next 4 years, because the firm has an abundance of tax credits to carry forward. Finally, Western Capital views lease investments such as this as an alternative to lending, so if it does not write the lease, it will lend the $275 000 that would have been invested in the lease to some other party in the form of a term loan that would earn 10 percent before taxes.

Joan Haddad has always had the final say on all of Bunbury's lease-versus-purchase decisions, but the actual analysis of the relevant data is conducted by Bunbury's assistant treasurer, David Gillis. Traditionally, Bunbury's method of evaluating lease decisions has been to calculate the "present-value cost" of the lease payments versus the present value of the total charges if the equipment is purchased. However, in a recent evaluation, Haddad and Gillis got into a heated discussion about the appropriate discount rate to use in determining the present-value costs of leasing and of purchasing. The following points of view were expressed:

(1) Haddad argued that the discount rate should be the firm's weighted average cost of capital. She believed that a lease-versus-purchase decision was, in effect, a capital budgeting decision, and, as such, it should be evaluated at the company's cost of capital. In other words, one method or the other will provide a net cash savings in any year, and the dollars saved using the most advantageous method will be invested to yield the firm's cost of capital. Therefore, the average cost of capital is the appropriate opportunity rate to use in evaluating lease-versus-purchase decisions.

(2) Gillis, on the other hand, believed that the cash flows generated in a lease-versus-purchase situation are more certain than are the cash flows generated by the firm's average projects. Consequently, these cash flows should be discounted at a lower rate because of their lower risk. At the present time, the firm's cost of secured debt reflects the lowest risk rate to Bunbury. Therefore, 10 percent should be used as the discount rate in the lease-versus-purchase decision.

   To settle the debate, Haddad and Gillis asked the firm's external accountants to review the situation and to advise them on which discount rate was appropriate. This led to even more confusion because the firm's accountants, Ramesh Kumar and Brent Wilson, were also unable to reach agreement on which rate to use. Kumar, on the one hand, agreed with Haddad that the discount rate should be based on the average cost of capital, but on the grounds that leasing is simply an alternative to other means of financing. Leasing is a substitute for "financing," which is a mix of debt and equity, and it saves the cost of raising capital; this cost is the firm's weighted average cost of capital. Wilson, on the other hand, thought that none of the discount rates mentioned so far adequately accounted for the tax effects inherent in any capital budgeting decision, and he suggested the use of an after-tax cost of secured debt.

In the last lease-versus-purchase decision, the average cost of capital (13 percent) was used, but now Haddad is uncertain about the validity of this procedure. She is beginning to lean toward Brent Wilson's alternative, but she wonders if it would be appropriate to use a low-risk discount rate for evaluating all the cash flows in the analysis. Haddad is particularly concerned about the risk of the expected residual value. While the company is almost certain of the other cash flows and the tax shelters, the salvage value at the end of the fourth year is relatively uncertain, having a distribution of possible outcomes that makes its risk comparable to that of the average capital budgeting project undertaken by the firm. She is also concerned that using a discount rate based on the after-tax cost of a secured loan might be inappropriate when the funds used to purchase the equipment would come from internal sources. Perhaps the cost of equity capital also deserves consideration, because the funds could be used to increase the next quarterly dividend payment.

Questions

PART A: Lessee's Analysis

1. The conventional format for analyzing lease-versus-purchase decisions assumes that the money to buy the equipment will be obtained by borrowing. In this case, however, Bunbury has sufficient internally generated capital, held in the form of marketable securities, to buy the equipment outright. What impact does this have on the analysis?

2. Should Bunbury lease or purchase the equipment? Assume that if the decision is made to purchase the machine, it will be sold for its UCC on the first day of Year 5, and hence the full Year 4 CCA can be taken. However, this residual value should be considered a Year 4 cash inflow. Further, use the 6 percent after-tax cost of debt as the residual value discount rate. (Hint: Use Part A of Table 1 as a guide.)

3. Justify the discount rates that you used in the calculation process. Now assume that Haddad wants you to adjust the analysis to reflect the differential residual value risk. What impact does this have on the lease-versus-purchase decision? (Hint: The 13 percent cost of capital used to evaluate average risk projects is an *after-tax* cost.)

4. **a.** Based on the information given in the case, would you classify this lease as a financial lease or as an operating lease? For accounting purposes, a lease is classified as a financial lease, and hence must be capitalized and shown directly on the balance sheet, if the contract meets any one of the following conditions:
   (1) The lessee can buy the asset at the end of the lease term for a bargain price.
   (2) The lease transfers ownership to the lessee before the lease expires.
   (3) The lease lasts for 75 percent or more of the asset's estimated useful life.
   (4) The present value of the lease payments is 90 percent or more of the asset's value.
   b. Does the differential accounting treatment of operating-versus-financial leases make comparative financial statement analysis more difficult for outside financial analysts? If so, how might analysts overcome the problem?

5. In some instances, a company might be able to lease assets at a cost less than the cost the firm would incur if it financed the purchase with a loan. If the equipment represented a significant addition to the lessee's assets, could this affect its overall cost of capital, and hence the capital budgeting decision that preceded the lease analysis? Would this affect capital budgeting decisions related to other assets? Explain.

6. Now assume that Haddad estimates that the residual value could be as low as $0 or as high as $174 540. Further, she subjectively assigns a probability of occurrence of 0.25 to the extreme values and 0.50 to the base-case value, $87 470. Describe how Haddad's estimates could be incorporated into the analysis. If you are using the *Lotus* model, calculate Bunbury's net advantage to leasing (NAL) at each residual value. What is the expected NAL? (For this analysis, assume a 10 percent pre-tax discount rate on all cash flows.) To simplify your analysis, assume any difference between the salvage value and the undepreciated capital cost of the asset is taxed as recapture or a terminal loss.

PART B: Lessor's Analysis

7. Now evaluate the proposed lease from the point of view of the lessor, Western Capital. Assume that the residual value is equal to the UCC at the end of the fourth year, and use a 10 percent discount rate for all cash flows. Are the current terms favourable to Western? (Hint: Use Part B of Table 1 as a guide.)

PART C: Combined Analysis

8. Based on a 4-year use of the asset and a 10 percent pre-tax discount rate for all cash flows (i.e., the original conditions), you should have found that the lease is advantageous to both Bunbury and Western Capital. Can you identify a range of lease payments that would be profitable to both the lessor and the lessee? At which end of the range do you think the actual payment would be set? If you are using the *Lotus* model, specify the actual range of payments.

9. There is a possibility that Bunbury will move to its new production facility earlier than anticipated, and hence prior to the expiration of the lease. Thus, Haddad is considering asking Western Capital to include a cancellation clause in the lease contract. What impact would a cancellation clause have on the riskiness of the lease to Bunbury? How would it affect the risk to Western Capital? If you were Western Capital's leasing manager, would you change the lease terms if a cancellation clause were added? If so, what changes might be made?

10. Leases are sometimes written so that the lessee makes payments at the end of each year rather than in advance. If the lessor structured the analysis with deferred payments, how would this affect (a) the NAL from the lessee's standpoint and (b) the rate of return earned by the lessor? Could the lease payments be adjusted, if they were made on a deferred basis, to produce the same NAL as existed when payments were made in advance?

11. Assume now that Western Capital has no tax credits to carry forward, and hence is in the 40 percent tax bracket. Also assume that both parties to the lease estimate a $87 470 residual value and discount it at a 6.0 percent after-tax discount rate. In Question 2 you found Bunbury's NAL to be $2374. What do you think would happen to Western Capital's NPV under these conditions? If you are using the *Lotus* model, do the calculation.

12. What effect do you think Bunbury's tax rate has on its lease-versus-purchase decision? If you are using the *Lotus* model, find Bunbury's NAL at tax rates of 0, 10, 20, 30, 40, and 50 percent. Explain your results.

Table 1
Selected Cash Flow Data
(in Thousands of Dollars)

Capital Cost Allowance Table

Year	CCA Rate	Beginning UCC	CCA	Ending UCC
1	15%	$300.00	$ 45.00	$255.00
2	30	X	X	X
3	30	178.50	X	X
4	30	124.95	37.49	87.47
5	30	87.47	26.24	61.23
6	30	61.23	18.37	42.86
			$257.14	

Part A: Lessee's Analysis

Cost of Owning:

	Year 0	Year 1	Year 2	Year 3	Year 4
Equipment cost	($300.00)				
Maintenance	(15.00)	($15.00)	X	($15.00)	
Maintenance tax savings	6.00	6.00	X	6.00	
CCA tax shield		18.00	X	21.42	$14.99
Residual value					87.47
Residual value tax					0.00
Net owning cash flow	($309.00)	$ 9.00	X	($12.42)	($102.46)

Cost of Leasing:

	Year 0	Year 1	Year 2	Year 3	Year 4
Lease payment	($85.00)	($85.00)	X	($85.00)	
Payment tax savings	34.00	34.00	X	34.00	
Net leasing cash flow	($51.00)	($51.00)	X	($51.00)	$ 0.00

Part B: Lessor's Analysis

	Year 0	Year 1	Year 2	Year 3	Year 4
Equipment cost	($300.00)				
Maintenance	(15.00)	($15.00)	X	($15.00)	
Maintenance tax savings	0.00	0.00	X	0.00	
CCA tax shield	0.00	X	X	0.00	$ 0.00
Residual value					87.47
Residual value tax					0.00
Lease payment	85.00	85.00	X	85.00	
Lease payment tax	0.00	0.00	X	0.00	
	($230.00)	$70.00	X	$70.00	$87.47

15

Weaver Foods, Inc.

"Regardless of the reaction in the stock and bond markets," said Robert MacDougall, treasurer of Weaver Foods, Inc., "we must still raise $75 million of external capital next year. We've already contracted for the construction of the new plant, and penalty payments would be horrendous if we cancelled. Besides, if we are going to maintain our market position, we simply must continue our expansion program. I know money is expensive, but the investment dealers tell me we can cut our costs by issuing convertibles or bonds with warrants." MacDougall's remarks were directed to Weaver Foods' board of directors. The topic under consideration was how Weaver would raise $75 million in 1991 to finance a major plant expansion, which is a key element in the company's long-term modernization and expansion plan. Weaver had already committed to the construction program, and the contracts for this phase had been signed several months ago.

Weaver Foods is one of the largest producers of health foods in Canada, with a product line including everything from high-fibre cereals to vitamin supplements. Most of its products are packaged for grocery chains and sold under the stores' labels, and the remainder are sold as generic products. Like many packaged foods companies, however, Weaver's financial condition has deteriorated significantly over the last 5 years due to higher ingredient costs, and the firm's debt-to-capitalization ratio (short-term plus long-term debt, divided by total permanent capital, all at market value) has been steadily rising in the face of declining earnings. These events have caused Weaver's interest coverage ratio to fall to a dangerously low 2.7×, the firm's bonds to be downgraded from A to B⁺⁺, and the company's common stock to sell at only 70 percent of book value. (See Table 1 for Weaver's 1990 balance sheet.)

Its deteriorating financial situation has reduced the company's flexibility in obtaining external capital. Weaver had originally planned to issue first-mortgage bonds and to meet its equity requirements for the expansion in 1991 by retaining earnings. However, given the firm's low interest coverage,

Table 1
Balance Sheet for Year Ended
December 31, 1990

Assets	
Cash	$ 7 000 000
Accounts receivable	17 300 000
Materials and supplies	45 850 000
Total current assets	$ 70 150 000
Plant and equipment (net)	541 790 000
Total assets	$611 940 000
Claims on Assets	
Accounts payable	$ 14 500 000
Accruals	9 580 000
Notes payable[a]	45 000 000
Total current liabilities	$ 69 080 000
Long-term debt[b]	275 000 000
Total liabilities	$344 080 000
Common stock[c]	85 980 000
Retained earnings	181 880 000
Total common equity	$267 860 000
Total claims on assets	$611 940 000

[a] Unlike many companies, Weaver uses short-term notes payable as a source of permanent financing. Weaver's notes payable currently carry an interest cost of 8 percent and are valued at par.

[b] Weaver's outstanding bonds have a par value of $1000, a remaining life of 15 years, a coupon rate of 8 percent, and pay annual interest. These are first-mortgage bonds, and the current rate of interest for 15-year bonds with Weaver's rating is 10 percent.

[c] The current price of the company's common stock is $18.75 per share, and there are 10 million shares outstanding.

a new long-term debt issue at this time would almost certainly cause Weaver's credit rating to be downgraded again, which would relegate its bonds to the junk category. Additionally, the capital structure currently employed by Weaver is based on the cost figures developed by the firm's investment dealers (see Table 2). These data indicate that Weaver could expect a significant increase in its weighted average cost of capital if management increased the use of leverage at this time.

Management is also unwilling to issue new common stock at this time, both because of the depressed share price and because of the dilution in book value and earnings per share that would occur if it sold stock at a price below book value. Finally, Weaver's board has always refused to issue preferred stock because (1) preferred dividends, which the board regards as being similar to interest payments, are nondeductible; (2) preferred stock is riskier to investors than debt, and thus preferred has a relatively high rate of return;

Table 2
Assumed Relationships between Leverage and the Cost of Capital

Leverage (Long-Term Debt/Capital)	Short-Term Interest Rate	Long-Term Interest Rate	Cost of Retained Earnings	Cost of New Common Stock
0.0%	7.00%	9.00%	12.00%	12.80%
10.0	7.20	9.25	12.10	12.90
20.0	7.40	9.50	12.50	13.30
30.0	7.60	9.70	12.90	13.80
40.0	7.80	9.90	13.80	14.75
50.0(Target)	8.00	10.00	15.60	16.80
60.0	9.00	12.00	1ᶜ 00	19.80
70.0	12.00	15.00	21.60	23.40

Note: The numbers presented here assume that the short-term debt/total capitalization ratio remains constant at the predetermined optimal amount. Also, capital is defined here as notes payable plus long-term debt plus equity.

and (3) the company would be unable to pay common stock dividends if the preferred dividends had to be eliminated.

Thus, MacDougall felt that the only viable alternatives available to Weaver were either convertible bonds or bonds with warrants. Based on several discussions with Weaver's investment dealers, MacDougall has tentatively concluded that the firm could raise the required $75 million by selling one of three alternative issues. First, the company could sell 7 percent, annual-payment, convertible debentures, with a par value of $1000 and convertible into 50 shares of common stock. This issue would mature in 25 years, and it would be callable on any interest payment date after 2 years, with an initial call premium of $70 per bond that would decline by $70/23 = $3.04 per year thereafter. Alternatively, Weaver could issue 9 percent, $1000 par value, annual-payment debentures, which would be convertible into 40 shares of common stock. This issue would also have a maturity of 25 years, and it would again be callable on any interest payment date after 2 years, at a call premium of $90 in Year 2 but declining by $3.91 per year after Year 2. Finally, Weaver could issue 8 percent, annual-payment debentures carrying 80 detachable warrants to buy a share of common stock at $20 each. These bonds would have a par value of $1000 and would mature in 25 years, and the warrants would expire in 6 years if they had not been exercised. MacDougall does not regard these rates as firm; they might have to be adjusted on the basis of further analysis.

Since both of the convertible issues, and also the bonds with warrants, would be subordinated debentures, they would stand behind the firm's existing mortgage bonds in the event of bankruptcy. Weaver's outstanding mortgage bonds only have a B⁺⁺ rating, so its convertibles or bonds with warrants would probably be rated B⁺. Currently, B⁺ bonds, with a maturity similar to that of convertibles or bonds with warrants, yield, on average, 11 percent. Therefore, the "pure bond value" of either the convertibles or the bonds with warrants would be determined by discounting at 11 percent.

As the directors' meeting was winding to a close, MacDougall was asked to thoroughly evaluate each of the financing alternatives and to develop a recommendation for the next board meeting. As part of his analysis, Mac-Dougall was asked to calculate the firm's weighted average cost of capital (WACC) under each of the financing choices. The WACC is found using the following equation:

$$\text{WACC} = w_{dST}k_{dST}(1 - T) + w_{dLT}k_{dLT}(1 - T) + w_s(k_s \text{ or } k_e).$$

Here

w_{dST} = weight assigned to short-term debt
k_{dST} = cost of new short-term debt.
w_{dLT} = weight assigned to long-term debt.
k_{dLT} = cost of new long-term debt.
T = marginal tax rate.
w_s = weight assigned to equity.
k_s = cost of retained earnings.
k_e = cost of new common stock.

The weights in the preceding equation are *market value* weights, not *book value* weights. To include either of the convertible issues or the bonds with warrants in the analysis, the term $w_c k_c$ would have to be added to the equation. Here, w_c is the proportion of capital obtained in the form of convertibles or warrants, and k_c is the cost of convertible capital or the cost of capital using warrants. To determine the cost of convertible capital or of capital using warrants (k_c), MacDougall will have to make an assumption about when the bonds will be converted or the warrants exercised.

Your task is to assist MacDougall in preparing his report by answering the following questions.

Questions

1. **a.** Calculate Weaver's current market value capital structure. In your calculations, ignore the relatively minor amounts of spontaneously generated liabilities, but do include notes payable, because Weaver uses them as a permanent source of capital.

   b. Determine Weaver's current weighted average cost of capital based on the cost data and WACC equation given in the case. In your calculations, use the cost of new common stock given in Table 2 for the cost of equity.

Figure 1
Graphic Model of a Convertible Bond

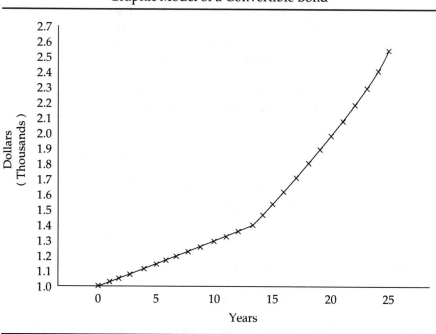

2. For the 9 percent convertible issue, replace the Xs in Table 3, and use these data to construct a graph (i.e., complete Figure 1) showing the conversion value, bond value, call price, and maturity value of this issue over time. In answering this question, assume that Weaver's stock price will grow at a rate of 5 percent per year for the foreseeable future.

3. Once a convertible becomes callable, what factors would influence a company's decision to call the issue as opposed to letting it remain outstanding? What factors would induce the holders of a convertible to convert voluntarily?

4. Assume that Weaver would call the 9 percent convertible issue after the first interest payment date on which the conversion value of the bond is 40 percent greater than the bond's par value. According to the assumptions embodied in Figure 1, in what year should the bond be called for conversion? (Hint: Set C_t = par value × 1.4, and find the value of t that forces equality.) Note that the 7 percent convertible issue would be called in 9 years under the same set of assumptions.

5. For this and the next question, assume that your answer to Question 4 was $n = 13$, the number of years to conversion, regardless of your actual

answer. What is the after-tax cost to Weaver of the 9 percent convertible issue? For the 7 percent issue, k_c is 7.86 percent if conversion occurs in Year 9; this value is calculated as follows:

Given the equation

$$M = \sum_{t=1}^{n} \frac{I(1-T)}{(1+k_c)^t} + \frac{P_n CR}{(1+k_c)^n},$$

where

M = market value of bond = $1000.
n = number of years to conversion = 9.
I = interest in dollars = $70.
T = tax rate = 0.40.
P_n = expected market price of stock at the end of period n
    = $18.75(1.05)^9$ = $29.09.
CR = conversion ratio = 50.

Then,

$$\$1000 = \sum_{t=1}^{9} \frac{\$70(1-0.4)}{(1+k_c)^t} + \frac{\$29.09(50)}{(1+k_c)^9}$$

$$\$1000 = \$42.00(\text{PVIFA}_{k_c,9}) + \$1454.50(\text{PVIF}_{k_c,9})$$

$$k_c = 7.86\%.$$

6. What is the expected before-tax rate of return to investors on the 9 percent convertible issue, assuming a call in Year 13? What accounts for the difference between the investor's return and the company's cost on the same issue? Assuming a call in Year 9, the expected before-tax rate of return on the 7 percent convertible issue is 10.30 percent.

7. What would Weaver's weighted average cost of capital be if it issues $75 million of the 9 percent convertible bonds? In your calculation, assume that all new equity is raised as retained earnings. Even though the capital structure weights will necessarily change due to the addition of $75 million of convertibles, assume that the costs of notes payable, long-term debt, and common stock do not change; that is, use k_{dST} = 8%, k_{dLT} = 10%, and k_s = 15.6%. (Note: k_a = WACC = 9.49 percent if the 7 percent convertibles are used.) Do you think it is reasonable to assume that the component costs would remain constant? If not, how would they be likely to change?

8. A graphic model of the market value of the convertible is shown in Figure 1. According to Table 3, the market value of the convertible in Year 10 is $1306. Suppose you purchased 10 bonds at $1306, and then the next day the company called the bonds for conversion. How much

would you gain or lose? What does this suggest about the market value line; that is, is the market value line in the graph consistent with the other data, and is it drawn correctly? Explain.

9. Calculate the after-tax cost to the company of the bonds with warrants. The before-tax yield to investors is 10.58 percent, calculated as follows:
   (1) The straight-debt value of the bond is

$$V_B \sum_{t=1}^{25} \frac{\$80}{(1.11)^t} + \frac{\$1000}{(1.11)^{25}} = \$747.35.$$

   (2) Therefore, the value of the warrants must be

   $$V_W = \$1000 - \$747.35 = \$252.65, \text{ or}$$
   $$\$252.65/80 = \$3.16 \text{ per warrant.}$$

   (3) The expected stock price in 6 years is $18.75(1.05)^6 = \$25.13$. With an exercise price of $20, the expected value of the warrants in 6 years is $5.13, for a total value of $5.13(80) = \$410.40 \approx \$410$.
   (4) Thus an investor faces this cash flow stream:

0	1	2	3	4	5	6	7	24	25
−$1000	$80	$80	$80	$80	$80	$ 80	$80	$80	$ 80
						410			1000
						$490			$1080

With a financial calculator, we find the IRR of this stream to be 10.58 percent, so k_w to investors = 10.58 percent before taxes.

10. Do you think investors would be willing to pay par value for the warrant and for the two convertible issues? If you think that any of the securities would be overvalued or undervalued at an initial price of $1000, how might the terms of the various issues be changed to make them "more reasonable?"

11. Based on your analysis up to this point, what recommendation should MacDougall make to Weaver's board of directors regarding the financing alternatives?

12. Assume that Weaver changes the coupon rate on the 9 percent convertible issue to 9.5 percent. Also, it changes the call premium in Year 2 to $95, and this premium will fall by $4.13 each year. If you are not using the *Lotus* model, discuss how these changes would affect the company's cost and investors' return. If you are using the model, quantify the

after-tax cost to the company and the before-tax return to investors for this issue. What would the company's weighted average cost of capital be with this issue?

Table 3
Conversion and Bond Values
for 9 Percent Convertible Bonds

Year	Conversion Value[a]	Bond Value[b]	Call Price[c]	Maturity Value	Estimated Market Value[d]
0	$ 750	$ 832	$1090	$1000	$1000
5	957	841	1078	1000	1143
10	X	X	X	1000	1306
15	1559	882	1039	1000	1559
20	1990	926	1020	1000	1990
25	2540	1000	1000	1000	2540

[a]Conversion value = $C_t = P_0(1 + g)^t R$,

where
t = years since issue date.
P_0 = initial stock price.
g = growth rate in stock price.
R = conversion ratio.

Example for Year 5: $C_5 = \$18.75(1 + 0.05)^5 40 = \$23.93(40) = \$957$.

[b]Bond value = $B_t = \sum_{j=1}^{n} \dfrac{I}{(1 + k_d)^j} + \dfrac{M}{(1 + k_d)^n} = I(\text{PVIF}_{k_d,}n) + M(\text{PVIF}_{k_d,}n)$,

where
n = number of years remaining until maturity.
j = time subscript from 1 to n.
k_d = market rate of interest of equivalent risk, nonconvertible debt issue.
I = dollars of interest paid each year.
M = maturity value.

Example for Year 5: $B_5 = \$90 \,(\text{PVIFA}_{11\%,20}) + \$1000(\text{PVIF}_{11\%,20}) = \$841$.

[c]The bond is not callable for the first 2 years. After Year 2, the call premium is reduced by a constant amount each year to result in a zero call premium at maturity; that is, the premium is reduced by $\frac{1}{23}(\$90) = \$3.91$ per year.

Example for Year 5: $\$1090 - 3(\$3.91) = \$1078$.

[d]The market value estimates were obtained by first determining the year in which conversion is expected to occur (see Question 4). At that time, and in subsequent years, the market value should be equal to the conversion value. For years prior to conversion, we found the growth rate that would equate the initial market value, $1000, with the conversion value at the expected date of conversion. In this instance, the growth rate was found to be 2.7%.

Example for Year 5: MV = $\$1000(1 + 0.027)^5 = \$1143$.

VII

Working Capital Management

Case 16
Working Capital Policy and Financing Kelsey Furniture Company

Case 17
Inventory Management LakeSide Marine Corporation

Case 18
Cash Budgeting MacAdam Enterprises

Case 19
Credit Policy Kiddyland Clothes, Inc.

16

Kelsey Furniture Company

Kelsey Furniture is a medium-sized manufacturer of metal file cabinets for home and office use. The company sells its office furniture through regular channels, but its home products are sold through mass merchandisers such as Kmart under the trade name "Office Friends." Sales of both lines have grown substantially over the past 20 years because of the increasing demand for storage containers. Because the demand for paper storage appears to be slowing, Kelsey has recently moved into the manufacture and distribution of computer tape and diskette storage systems, which it believes to be the "hot" growth area of the future.

Although the firm has always been up to date in manufacturing and marketing, financial management has tended to take a back seat. In fact, the recently retired financial manager joined the company right out of high school, and he worked his way up from an initial position of mail clerk. To revitalize the finance function, the company brought in Rob Lindstrom, who had worked for several years at a competing company, to be the chief financial officer (CFO).

After spending several weeks familiarizing himself with Kelsey's operations, Lindstrom concluded that one of his first tasks should be to develop a rational working capital policy. With this in mind, he decided to examine three alternative policies: (1) an *aggressive* policy, which calls for minimizing the amount of cash and inventories held, and for using only short-term debt; (2) a *conservative* policy, which calls for holding relatively large amounts of cash and inventories, and for using only long-term debt; and (3) a *moderate* policy, which falls between the two extremes. The aggressive policy would

Table 1
Estimated Balance Sheets

| | Alternative Working Capital Policies | | |
	Aggressive	Moderate	Conservative
Current assets	$4 000 000	$ 5 000 000	$ 6 000 000
Net fixed assets	5 000 000	5 000 000	5 000 000
Total assets	$9 000 000	$10 000 000	$11 000 000
Short-term debt	$4 500 000	$ 2 500 000	$ 0
Long-term debt	0	2 500 000	5 500 000
Total equity	4 500 000	5 000 000	5 500 000
Total claims	$9 000 000	$10 000 000	$11 000 000

result in the smallest investment in net working capital (current assets minus current liabilities).

Lindstrom tentatively plans to hold the level of accounts receivable constant; i.e., it would be the same under each of the three policies. Tom Critchley, the company's president, suggested that as a part of the aggressive policy, where cash and inventories are minimized, the company could also minimize accounts receivable, and vice versa, under the conservative policy. However, Lindstrom is bothered by calling a policy, under which accounts receivable are allowed to rise, "conservative." After all, the actions that would cause receivables to rise (while holding sales constant) would include lengthening credit terms and selling on credit to weaker customers, and neither of those actions seems "conservative." Still, Lindstrom knows that Critchley will bring this point up when they discuss the merits of the three policies in the board of directors meeting, when the directors will be asked to approve one of the policies.

Lindstrom also concluded that the company's $5 million of net fixed assets are sufficient to accommodate a relatively wide range of sales, so fixed assets can remain constant regardless of what is done in the working capital area. As for current assets, Table 1 contains Lindstrom's estimates of the firm's balance sheet under the three alternative working capital policies. Kelsey's stock sells at about its book value, and the company's target capital structure calls for a debt ratio in the range of 45 to 55 percent, so all three working capital policies are consistent with Kelsey's target debt/equity mix. In fact, all three alternatives have a 50/50 debt/equity mix, and hence the decision does not affect the mix of debt and equity but, rather, the level of the current assets and the maturity structure of the debt. Lindstrom's best estimate of debt costs is 10 percent for short-term debt and 13 percent for long-term debt.

The choice of working capital policy will affect some of the company's costs. Thus, while variable costs are expected to be 50 percent of sales

Table 2
Estimated Sales under Each Working Capital Policy

Economy	Working Capital Policy		
	Aggressive	Moderate	Conservative
Weak	$ 9 000 000	$11 000 000	$13 000 000
Average	12 000 000	13 000 000	14 000 000
Strong	13 000 000	14 500 000	16 000 000

regardless of which working capital policy is adopted, fixed costs are likely to be a function of the level of current assets held—the greater the level of current assets, the greater the fixed costs. This situation results primarily from the need to hold the larger inventories in high-cost, dehumidified warehouses, and because of higher insurance costs. Lindstrom estimates annual fixed costs to be $4 000 000 under the aggressive policy, $4 500 000 under the moderate policy, and $5 000 000 with the conservative policy. Kelsey's federal-plus-provincial tax rate is 40 percent.

Working capital policy will also affect the firm's ability to respond to varying economic conditions. In an average economy, Kelsey's sales would be highest if the firm used a conservative policy. Here the firm's inventories would be the highest, so it could respond immediately to incoming orders and hence not risk losing sales because of stockouts. Kelsey's cash and marketable securities would also be highest under a conservative policy. Further, if higher sales occurred because of the conservative policy, then accounts receivable would also be higher, even if credit standards and credit terms were not changed.[1] Conversely, expected sales are lowest under an aggressive policy. Here the firm would have low cash and inventory levels, and hence some sales would be lost, which would depress the level of receivables.

The different policies would also cause sales to react differently to changing economic conditions. In a strong economy, the conservative approach with its higher inventories would be best for generating increased sales. On the other hand, an aggressive policy would inhibit the firm from responding to increased demand. Table 2 contains Lindstrom's best estimates of the sales levels under the alternative policies for three different states of the economy.

---

1 Note that working capital policy actually consists of two independent decisions: (1) the level of current assets, and (2) the way in which the current assets are financed. In this case, to simplify the numerical analysis, the two independent decisions are treated as dependent. Thus, a conservative policy implies a conservative financing policy, along with large holdings of current assets. Similarly, an aggressive policy signifies a heavy use of short-term debt along with relatively small holdings of current assets.

With these estimates in mind, Lindstrom must now draft a report to present to Tom Critchley and Kelsey's Board of Directors. Assume that you are Lindstrom's assistant, and he has asked you to help him prepare the report. To help you get started, Lindstrom has generated the following list of questions. Your task now is to answer them, after which you must help Lindstrom prepare the final report. Since you were hired by the previous CFO, you know that Lindstrom does not have too much confidence in your knowledge or ability. This assignment will give you a chance to prove your worth—in effect, your performance will start you on the path to the top—or out the door—so you really need to get it right.

Questions

1. The two most basic decisions concerning working capital policy relate to the level of current assets and the manner in which current assets are financed. Explain the differences between aggressive, moderate, and conservative working capital policies in these two areas.

2. Rob Lindstrom expresses some doubts as to how to characterize accounts receivable in terms of conservative, moderate, or aggressive working capital policies. Obviously, the higher the level of sales, the higher the level of accounts receivable will be. On the other hand, if the firm takes deliberate actions that raise the level of receivables as a percentage of sales, would you characterize those actions as aggressive or conservative? Clearly, if the company takes the action of keeping more cash or inventories on hand, that is a conservative action, but is an action that raises receivables conservative? Explain.

3. Construct pro forma income statements for each working capital policy under an average economy, a weak economy, and a strong economy. Then, use these data to calculate ROEs and basic earning power ratios (EBIT/Total assets). (Table 3 shows a partially completed worksheet.) How could these data be used to help decide on the optimal working capital policy? Could you choose a working capital policy on the basis of the information generated thus far?

4. Assume that there is a 50 percent chance of an average economy, a 25 percent chance of a weak economy, and a 25 percent chance of a strong economy. What is the expected ROE under each policy? How do the policies compare in terms of relative riskiness? (Hint: Riskiness can be expressed in terms of standard deviation [σ] and coefficient of variation [CV].)

5. Now assume that the Bank of Canada, reacting to increasing inflationary pressures, tightens monetary policy shortly after Kelsey has made its working capital policy decision. Any long-term debt outstanding would

be locked in at 13 percent, but Kelsey would have to roll over any short-term debt outstanding at the new rate, which has skyrocketed to 15 percent. Assuming an average economy, what would be the resulting ROE under each policy? Do these results affect your previous conclusions about the relative riskiness of the three alternatives?

6. Like most companies of its size, Kelsey has two primary sources of short-term debt: trade credit and bank loans. One supplier, which furnishes Kelsey with $500 000 (gross) of materials a year, offers terms of 3/10, net 60.
   a. What are Kelsey's net daily purchases from this supplier? (Use a 360-day year.)
   b. What is the average level of Kelsey's accounts payable to this supplier, assuming the discount is taken? What is the average payables balance if the discount is not taken? What are the dollar amounts of free credit and costly credit from this supplier?
   c. What is the approximate percentage cost of the costly credit? What is the effective annual percentage cost?
   d. What conclusions do you reach from this analysis?

7. In discussing a possible loan with the firm's banker, Lindstrom learned that the bank would be willing to lend Kelsey up to $5 000 000 for one year at a 10 percent nominal, or stated, rate. However, Lindstrom failed to ask the banker about the specific terms of the loan. Assume that Kelsey will borrow $2 500 000.
   a. What would the effective interest rate be on the loan if it was a simple interest loan? If the banker offered to lend the money for 6 months, but with a guaranteed renewal at the same 10 percent simple interest rate, would this be as good as, better than, or worse than a straight one-year loan at 10 percent simple interest? Explain.
   b. What would be the effective interest rate if the loan was a discount loan? What face amount would be needed to provide Kelsey with $2 500 000 of available funds?
   c. Assume now that the loan terms call for an instalment loan with add-on interest and 12 equal monthly payments, with the first payment due at the end of the first month. What would be Kelsey's monthly payments? What would be the approximate percentage cost of this loan? What would be its effective annual rate? Would this type of loan be suitable if Kelsey needs all of the money for the entire year? What type of asset is most suitably financed by an instalment-type loan?
   d. Now assume that the bank charges simple interest, but it requires a 20 percent compensating balance.
      (1) Suppose Kelsey does not carry any cash balances at that bank. How much would the firm have to borrow to obtain the needed

$2 500 000 while meeting its compensating balance require-
ment? What is the effective annual percentage rate on this loan?

(2) Now suppose Kelsey currently carries an average cash balance
of $75 000 at the bank, and that those funds can be used as a part
of the compensating balance requirement. What effect does this
have on the amount borrowed, and on the effective cost of the
loan?

(3) Return to the scenario in which Kelsey currently maintains its
working cash balances in another bank. Now assume that the
bank from which Kelsey would borrow pays 5 percent simple
interest on all chequing account balances. What would be the
effective percentage cost of the loan in this situation?

e. Finally, assume that the bank charges discount interest, and it also
requires a 20 percent compensating balance. How much would
Kelsey have to borrow, and what would be the effective interest rate
under these conditions?

8. Assume now that you have had some additional discussions with Rob
Lindstrom, in which he told you that he would like more information
on the ROE and the riskiness of the alternative working capital policies
under different sets of assumptions. For example, he asked you to
assume that sales are independent of working capital policy, and then
to determine the expected ROE and standard deviation of ROE under
each policy if the sales estimates are $11 000 000 for a weak economy,
$13 000 000 for an average economy, and $14 500 000 for a strong economy. Similarly, he asked you to assume that a different manufacturing
process is used, causing the mix of fixed and variable costs to change.
Using the original sales estimate, he wanted to know what the expected
ROE and standard deviation of ROE would be under the three policies
if variable costs increased to 70 percent of sales (in all cases), and fixed
costs decreased to $1 000 000 under an aggressive policy, to $1 500 000
under the moderate policy, and to $2 000 000 under the conservative
policy. How would your answers to these questions, and similar questions, be used by top managers as they actually make the working capital
policy decision? Quantify your answer if you have access to the *Lotus*
1-2-3 model, but just discuss the situation if you do not.

9. What is your recommendation regarding a working capital policy for
Kelsey Furniture, and in what form should the company raise short-
term debt? You really do not have enough information to make a
definitive statement when answering this question, but assume that
Lindstrom wants you to at least make a preliminary recommendation,
which can be modified later if necessary.

Table 3
Pro Forma Income Statements

	Aggressive	Moderate	Conservative
Average Economy			
Sales	$12 000	$13 000	$14 000
Cost of goods sold	10 000	X	12 000
EBIT	$ 2 000	$ 2 000	$ 2 000
Interest on debt	450	X	715
EBT	$ 1 550	X	$ 1 285
Taxes	620	X	514
Net income	$ 930	X	$ 771
Basic earning power (EBIT/Assets)	22.2%	X	18.2%
Return on equity	20.7%	X	14.0%
Weak Economy			
Sales	$ 9 000	X	$13 000
Cost of good sold	8 500	X	11 500
EBIT	$ 500	X	$ 1 500
Interest on debt	450	X	715
EBT	$ 50	X	$ 785
Taxes	20	X	314
Net income	$ 30	X	$ 471
Basic earning power (EBIT/Assets)	5.6%	X	13.6%
Return on equity	0.7%	X	8.6%
Strong Economy			
Sales	$13 000	X	$16 000
Cost of good sold	10 500	X	13 000
EBIT	$ 2 500	X	$ 3 000
Interest on debt	450	X	715
EBT	$ 2 050	X	$ 2 285
Taxes	820	X	914
Net income	$ 1 230	X	$ 1 371
Basic earning power (EBIT/Assets)	27.8%	X	27.3%
Return on equity	27.3%	X	24.9%

17

---

*Inventory
Management*

LakeSide Marine
Corporation

LakeSide Marine manufactures fibreglass sailboats that range from 18-foot day sailers to 50-foot ocean racing yachts. The company was founded in Toronto, Ontario, but high labour costs forced it to move its manufacturing operations to Kingston, Ontario, in 1968. The boat building industry is very competitive and highly labour intensive, and profitability depends on getting the maximum efficiency out of the labour force. LakeSide has managed to keep its work force nonunionized, and this means that all of its employees can be shifted from task to task, thus allowing LakeSide to maintain flexibility. However, the price for this freedom has been a relatively high basic wage rate and a no-layoff policy. The no-layoff policy, in turn, makes it essential that the work force be kept productively employed, and this means that LakeSide must never run out of the various parts that go into the assembly of a boat. Therefore, the company must have a good inventory management system that can track a large and varied inventory of parts ranging from inboard diesel engines and masts costing thousands of dollars each to screws and rivets costing only pennies each.

Sailboats are built in sequential steps. First, the major fiberglass components are laid up in moulds. To begin, each mould is cleaned and inspected, and if no damage is found, the mould is waxed with an agent that facilitates lift-out of the finished work. Then gelcoat, the cosmetic outer layer, is sprayed into the mould and left to dry. If the gelcoat layer shows any imperfections, it must be destroyed, and LakeSide loses $50 to $500, depending on the size of the mould. If the gelcoat layer is good, fibreglass strips are laid by hand on top of the gelcoat and bonded with liquid resin until the desired thickness is reached. Some sections on the hulls of the large racing yachts have sections that exceed one inch in thickness, but most of the sections are only about ¼ inch thick. Finally, the sections that do not require

Table 1
Inventory Multiplier Values

Order Lead Time Multipliers		Stockout Consequence Multiplier	
Lead Time Class	**Lead Time Multiplier**	**Consequence Class**	**Stockout Multiplier**
0–2 days	0	Unimportant	1
3–7 days	1	Average	3
8–30 days	2	Critical	5
1–3 months	4		
4–6 months	8		
7–12 months	12		

significant strength are formed by a "chopper gun," which sprays fibreglass strands into the mould, rather than by using strips laid by hand.

After drying, the sections from the moulding room are trimmed and brought to the assembly line. Here, the decks and hulls are joined, and the inboard engines, electrical wiring, steering systems, and plumbing fixtures are installed. After the structural work has been completed, the woodwork is done. Finally, the deck hardware (winches, cleats, running lights, and so on) and the interior upholstery are installed.

After a last inspection, the boat is taken to a water testing facility where the engine and transmission are tested, and the boat is checked for leaks. Finally, the boat is cleaned, installed on a shipping cradle, and placed on a truck that delivers it to dealers throughout Canada and the United States.

It should be obvious why efficient inventory control is so important to LakeSide Marine. If stocks of gelcoat, fibreglass, or resin were to run out, the moulding room would be forced to shut down, and input to the assembly line would be curtailed. Without engines, wiring harnesses, and steering systems, the boats could not progress to the finishing work stage. Any disruption in production would slow shipments to dealers and, possibly, result in missed sales. Further, since selling prices are fixed, any increase in production costs due to poor inventory control must be borne by the company, and the intense competition and resulting low profit margins makes this an almost intolerable situation.

LakeSide carries more than 10 000 different items in inventory, and these items vary widely in price, ordering lead times, and stockout costs. (Stockout costs are all the costs, from higher production costs to lost profits, that result from running out of stock of a particular item.) LakeSide uses the ABC method of inventory classification, along with a variety of inventory control methods, to manage its different inventory items. The ABC inventory classification system works like this: LakeSide maintains data on the average annual usage and cost of each item. Based on these data, plus the multiplier values given in Table 1, LakeSide assigns a numerical *inventory importance value* to each item by use of the following formula:

$$\text{Inventory importance value} = \left[\begin{array}{c}\text{Average} \\ \text{annual} \\ \text{usage}\end{array}\right] \times \left[\begin{array}{c}\text{Cost} \\ \text{per} \\ \text{unit}\end{array}\right] \times \left[\begin{array}{c}\text{Lead} \\ \text{time} \\ \text{multiplier}\end{array} + \begin{array}{c}\text{Stockout} \\ \text{multiplier}\end{array}\right].$$

For example, a customized 5-inch chrome-plated winch costs LakeSide $250, and the firm uses 1000 units per year. The winches require an order lead time of 10 days, and they are in the average-consequence class. Thus, the inventory importance value of the winches is $1 250 000:

Inventory importance value = (1000)($250)(2 + 3) = $1 250 000.

No particular significance can be attached to the $1 250 000—it is just a number used to compare the importance of this item with other inventory items.

Each of LakeSide's inventory items is analyzed similarly; the inventory importance values for the various items are arrayed from highest to lowest, each item's percentage of the total importance value is calculated, and then the *cumulative* percentage values are calculated. Finally, the items are separated into three classes, labelled A, B, and C. Ten percent of the inventory items—those in the A class—account for 50 percent of the total importance value, while 60 percent of the number of items are in the Class C, but these items constitute only 18 percent of the total importance value.

To better utilize its managerial time, LakeSide focuses most of its attention on the Class A items. For items in this class, LakeSide's financial manager reviews recent usage rates, stock position, and delivery time on a monthly basis, and adjusts the control and ordering system as necessary. Class B items are reviewed every quarter, while Class C items are only reviewed annually.

Even though this process has served LakeSide well, David Pelletier, the firm's newly hired financial manager, thinks the company is carrying excess inventories. He notes that LakeSide has never come close to having a stockout, even when boat orders required around-the-clock production and when supplier backlogs led to significant shipping delays. Pelletier believes that a thorough review should be undertaken of all Class A items, and that it might be possible to increase inventory turnover 25 percent by trimming current stocks. To convince LakeSide's president and CEO, Pelletier plans to focus initially on a single item—the 5-inch chrome-plated winch. Table 2 contains inventory cost and delivery data on this item.

LakeSide currently uses a single source for this item, Canadian Winches (Supplier A). Supplier A requires an $800 set-up fee on each order, in addition to the basic cost per unit, and it delivers in 10 days. Although the winches are basically standard items, LakeSide, as a top-of-the-line producer, customizes the winches with an imprint of the firm's logo. LakeSide is considering another supplier, Bronzeware, Inc. (Supplier B), which

Table 2
Cost and Usage Data:
Customized 5-Inch Chrome-Plated Winch

Expected annual usage	1000 units
Cost per unit	$250
Inventory carrying costs:	
Depreciation	1%
Storage and handling	8
Interest expense	10
Property taxes	2
Insurance	2
Total carrying costs	23%
Inventory ordering costs	
Supplier A	$1000
Supplier B	$500
Delivery lead times	
Supplier A	10 days
Supplier B	20 days

charges only a $300 set-up fee, but which takes 20 days to deliver. It costs LakeSide another $200 to process each order and to customize the winches, regardless of which supplier is used. Thus, the total order cost is $1000 for Supplier A and $500 for Supplier B.

Assume that you are Pelletier's assistant, and that he has asked you to look into the inventory situation. To give you direction, he prepared the following list of questions. Answer them, and then be prepared to discuss LakeSide's inventory situation with Pelletier and the management team.

Questions

1. What is the economic ordering quantity for standard 5-inch winches if they are ordered from (a) Supplier A, and (b) Supplier B? Round your answers up to the next whole unit, because LakeSide cannot order a fraction of a winch.

2. What assumptions are implied in the EOQ model? Do these assumptions appear reasonable when applied to LakeSide Marine?

3. a. How many orders should be placed each year if LakeSide buys from Supplier A? How many orders should be placed if the firm buys from Supplier B?

b. What is the reorder point (in units) for each supplier? Assume for now that no safety stocks are held, and use a 360-day year.

4. Calculate the total inventory cost (the cost of ordering plus the cost of carrying inventories) that LakeSide would incur from each supplier. On the basis of the information developed thus far, which supplier should LakeSide use?

5. LakeSide currently carries a safety stock of 75 winches to protect itself against stockouts due to delivery delays and/or an increase in the usage rate. However, if it decides to switch to Supplier B, LakeSide would need to increase the safety stock to 150 units to reflect Supplier B's longer lead time.
   a. Assuming that the desired safety stock is currently on hand, what is the total cost of ordering and carrying inventories, including the safety stock, using Supplier A? What is the cost of using Supplier B?
   b. How does the introduction of safety stocks affect the reorder points as calculated in Part b of Question 3?
   c. Assume that there is a shipping delay. How many days after an order is placed could LakeSide continue to operate at its expected usage rate before its entire stock of 5-inch winches is reduced to zero? Compute this figure for both Supplier A and Supplier B.

6. The cost of carrying inventories has been calculated using the current cost of bank loans (see Table 2). Do you think this is the appropriate rate? Explain, and in your answer consider both the WACC and tax effects.

7. LakeSide's production is relatively constant throughout the year, but if its sales and production were highly seasonal, could the EOQ model still be used? If so, would modifications be required? Explain.

8. Suppose Supplier A, the current supplier, offers a 2 percent discount on the $250 per unit purchase price on orders of 250 or more units. Should LakeSide take the quantity discount? (In answering this question, assume that LakeSide holds a 75-unit safety stock.)

9. What are some methods that LakeSide might use to control the inventory of 5-inch winches? That is, how can it keep track of the number of units in stock, and then be sure an order is placed when the order point is reached?

10. How much difference does it make in terms of total costs if the EOQ is followed exactly as opposed to letting orders vary 10 to 20 percent on either side of the EOQ? If you are using the *Lotus* model, provide some data to support your answer.

11. **a.** There is some question as to the proper cost of capital to be applied when estimating carrying costs. How sensitive is the EOQ to carrying costs if Supplier A is used? Put another way, does the cost of

capital used to obtain the EOQ make a large or only a small difference in terms of the resulting EOQ? If you are using the *Lotus* model, provide some data to support your answer, and show the effect of the changed EOQ and carrying costs on total costs.

b. How sensitive is EOQ to ordering costs, assuming a carrying cost of 23 percent is used? Again, if you are using the *Lotus* model, show the effect on total costs.

12. In many situations, companies are using just-in-time (JIT) inventory procedures with good results. What is involved in the JIT approach, and what factors would need to be considered before you could recommend that LakeSide adopt or not adopt a JIT system?

18

MacAdam Enterprises

Thomas Holbrook, the recently hired treasurer of MacAdam Enterprises, was summoned to the office of Cathryn MacAdam, the president and chief executive officer. When he got to MacAdam's office, Holbrook found her shuffling through a set of worksheets. She told him that because of a recent tightening of interest rates, and an impending shortage of loanable funds in the economy, the firm's bank had requested each of its major loan customers to provide it with an estimate of their borrowing requirements for the remainder of 1991 and 1992.

MacAdam had a previously scheduled meeting with her banker the following Monday, so she asked Holbrook to come up with an estimate of the firm's probable financing requirements for her to submit at that time. MacAdam was going away on a skiing expedition, a trip that had already been delayed several times, and she would not be back until just before her meeting with the banker.

MacAdam therefore asked Holbrook to prepare a cash budget while she was away. Due to the firm's rapid growth over the last few years, no one had taken the time to prepare a cash budget recently; thus, Holbrook was afraid he would have to start from scratch. From information already available, Holbrook knew that no loans would be needed from the bank before January, so he decided to restrict his budget to the period from January through June 1992. As a first step, he obtained the following sales forecast from the marketing department:

1991	November	$ 65 000
	December	90 000
1992	January	120 000
	February	150 000
	March	175 000
	April	200 000
	May	160 000
	June	105 000
	July	70 000
	August	55 000

(Note that the sales figures are *before* any discounts; that is, they are *not* net of discounts.)

MacAdam Enterprises' credit policy is 2/10, net 30, and hence a 2 percent discount is allowed if payment is made within 10 days of the sale. Otherwise, payment in full is due 30 days after the date of sale. On the basis of a previous study, Holbrook estimates that, generally, 15 percent of the firm's customers take the discount, 65 percent pay within 30 days, and 20 percent pay late, with the late payments averaging about 60 days after the invoice date. For monthly budgeting purposes, discount sales are assumed to be collected in the month of the sale, net sales in the month after the sale, and late sales 2 months after the sale.

MacAdam Enterprises begins production of goods 2 months before the anticipated sale date. Variable production costs are made up entirely of purchased materials and labour, which total 55 percent of forecasted sales— 15 percent for materials and 40 percent for labour. All materials are purchased just before production begins, or 2 months before the sale of the finished goods. On average, MacAdam Enterprises pays 45 percent of the materials cost in the month it receives the materials, and the remaining 55 percent the next month, or 1 month prior to the sale. Labour expenses follow a similar pattern, but only 30 percent is paid 2 months prior to sale, while 70 percent is paid 1 month before the sale.

MacAdam Enterprises pays fixed general and administrative expenses of approximately $22 000 a month, while lease obligations amount to $7500 per month. Both expenditures are expected to continue at the same level throughout the forecast period. The firm estimates miscellaneous expenses to be $6750 monthly, and fixed assets are currently being depreciated by $9000 per month. MacAdam Enterprises has $250 000 (book value) of bonds outstanding; they carry a 12 percent semiannual coupon, and interest is paid on January 15 and July 15. Also, the company is planning to replace an old machine in June with a new one costing $125 000. The old machine has both a zero book and a zero market value. Federal and provincial income taxes are expected to be $18 000 quarterly, and payments must be made on the 15th of December, March, June, and September. MacAdam Enterprises has a policy of maintaining a minimum cash balance of $70 000, and this amount will be on hand on January 1, 1992.

Assume that you were recently hired as Tom Holbrook's assistant, and he has turned the job of preparing the cash budget over to you. You must meet with him and Cathryn MacAdam on Sunday night to review the budget prior to her meeting with the banker on Monday. Answer the following questions, which he gave you to provide you with some direction, but also think about any other related issues that Holbrook or MacAdam, or the banker, might raise concerning the projections. In particular, be prepared to explain the sources of all the numbers, and the effects on the company's funds requirements if any of the basic assumptions turn out to be incorrect.

Your predecessor was fired for not really understanding a report he submitted, and you don't want to suffer the same fate!

Questions

1. Construct a monthly cash budget for MacAdam Enterprises for the period January through June 1992. For purposes of this question, disregard both interest payments on short-term bank loans and interest received from investing surplus funds. Also, assume that all cash flows occur on the 15th of each month. Finally, note that collections from sales in November and December of 1991 will not be completed until January and February of 1992, respectively. (Use Table 1 as a worksheet, replacing the Xs with numbers. If you have access to the *Lotus* model, complete the worksheet to generate the required numbers.) What is the maximum funds shortfall during the 6-month planning period?

2. Assume that the bank will agree to give MacAdam a $100 000 line of credit. Will this be sufficient to cover any expected cash shortfalls? Suppose the bank refused to grant the loan, and thus MacAdam had to obtain short-term financing from other sources. What other sources might be available?

3. The monthly cash budget that you have prepared assumes that all cash flows occur on the 15th of each month. Suppose MacAdam Enterprises' outflows tend to cluster at the beginning of the month, while collections tend to be heaviest toward the end of each month. How would this affect the validity of the monthly budget? What could be done to correct any inaccuracies that might result from the mismatch of inflows and outflows?

4. Now assume that you and Holbrook decide that you need to develop a daily cash budget for the month of January, based on the following assumptions. (Use Table 2 as a guide.)
   (1) Assume that MacAdam Enterprises normally operates 7 days a week; therefore, use 31 days for your January cash budget.
   (2) Sales are made at a constant rate throughout the month; that is, 1/31st of the January sales are made each day.
   (3) Daily sales follow the 15 percent, 65 percent, 20 percent collection breakdown.
   (4) Discount purchasers take full advantage of the 10-day discount period before paying, and "on time" purchasers wait the full 30 days to pay. Thus, collections during the first 10 days of January will reflect discount sales from the last 10 days of December, plus "regular" sales made in earlier months. Also, on January 31, Mac-

Adam will begin collecting January's net sales and December's late sales.

(5) The lease payment is made on the first of the month.

(6) Fifty percent of both labour costs and general and administrative expenses are paid on the 1st, and 50 percent are paid on the 15th.

(7) Materials are delivered on the 1st and paid for on the 5th.

(8) Miscellaneous expenses are incurred and paid evenly throughout the month; 1/31st each day.

(9) Required interest payments are made on the 15th.

(10) The target cash balance is $70 000, and this amount must be in the bank on each day. This minimum balance is required by the firm's contracts with the bank.

If you calculated it correctly, the monthly cash budget should have indicated that a maximum bank loan of $49 298 will be required in January. Does the daily cash budget support this conclusion?

5. Think about the mechanics of the bank loan. During a typical month, the funds needed or the cash surplus would be changing daily. Could the company increase or decrease its loan on a daily basis? If it could not, would this have any effect on the amount of funds that it needs?

6. You are aware that Cathryn MacAdam is concerned about the efficient utilization of her firm's cash resources. Specifically, she has questioned whether or not seasonal variations should be incorporated into the firm's target balance. In other words, during months when cash needs are greatest, the target balance would be somewhat higher, while the target would be set at a lower level during slack months. Would you recommend that MacAdam Enterprises follow this strategy? If the firm had any compensating balance requirements, would this affect your answer? How would a variable target balance be incorporated into the monthly cash budget? How would it be incorporated into the daily cash budget?

7. The only receipts shown in MacAdam Enterprises' cash budget are collections. What are some other types of inflows that could occur? Also, the budget ignored short-term interest expense and income; if MacAdam Enterprises paid interest at 7 percent on the short-term bank loan and received interest at 5 percent on surplus cash, how could these items be incorporated into the cash budget? Be specific; indicate exactly how the budget would be modified, and give an example.

8. Because cash is a nonearning asset, MacAdam Enterprises' cash management policy is to invest any surplus funds in marketable securities. Can you suggest an investment policy that will provide liquidity and safety, yet offer the firm a reasonable return on its investment? Specifically, describe the types of securities, the desired maturities, the expected returns, and the risks that would be involved. Would your

suggestions be the same for a company whose cash balances were projected to be in the millions of dollars as opposed to MacAdam Enterprises' thousands? Would it matter if the forecasts showed cash surpluses for all future months, going out indefinitely, versus a situation in which surpluses and deficits alternated from month to month due to seasonal factors?

9. The cash budget is a forecast, so most of the cash flows shown are expected values rather than amounts known with certainty. If actual sales, and hence collections, were different from the forecasted levels, then the forecasted surpluses and deficits would be incorrect. You know that Cathryn MacAdam and Tom Holbrook will be interested in knowing how various changes in the key assumptions would affect the funds surplus or deficit. For example, if sales fell below the forecasted level, what effect would that have? It would be particularly bad to have a $100 000 line of credit and then find that, due to incorrect assumptions, the actual cash requirement was $200 000!

   With this in mind, answer the following questions. If you are using the *Lotus* model, quantify your answers. Otherwise, just discuss the likely effects of the indicated changes. In both cases, indicate how the company should prepare for the types of events noted. In this discussion, recognize that getting a line of credit is not without cost—banks charge commitment fees that typically amount to 0.5 percent of the unused credit line.

   a. What would be the impact on the monthly net cash flows if actual sales from January through June 1992 were 20 percent *below* the forecasted amounts? In your answer, assume that purchases and labour, as well as all other expenses, are set by contract at the start of the 6-month forecast period on the basis of the original expected sales, so the outflows cannot be adjusted downward during the planning period even though sales decline below the forecasted levels.

   b. Would the $100 000 line of credit be sufficient if actual sales in January through June were only 50 percent of the forecasted level? To answer this question, again assume that all expenses are based on the expected level of sales, not the realized level.

   c. Suppose customers changed their payment patterns and began paying as follows: 10 percent in the month of sale, 20 percent in the following month, and 70 percent in the second month, versus the old 15-65-20 pattern. Now how large a credit line would the company require?

10. Based on all of your analysis, how large a credit line would you recommend that Cathryn MacAdam seek from her banker? If you find it difficult to identify a defendable number, what other information would you want, and how would you suggest the credit line be established?

Table 1
Monthly Cash Budget Worksheet

	November	December	January	February	March	April	May	June	July	August
I. Collections and Payments										
Gross sales (expected)	$65 000	X	X	X	X	X	$160 000	$105 000	$70 000	$55 000
Gross sales (realized)	$65 000	X	X	X	X	X	$160 000	$105 000	$70 000	$55 000
Collections:										
Month of sale	$ 9 555	$13 230	X	X	X	X	$ 23 520	$ 15 435		
1 month after sale		X	X	X	97 500	113 750	130 000	104 000		
2 months after sale			X	X	24 000	30 000	35 000	40 000		
Total collections			$89 140	$118 050	X	X	X	X		
Purchases	$18 000	X	X	X	$24 000	$ 15 750	$ 10 500	$ 8 250		
Payments:										
2 months prior to sale	8 100	10 125	11 813	X	X	X	X	X		
1 month prior to sale		9 900	12 375	14 438	X	X	X	X		
Total payments			$24 188	X	X	X	X	$ 9 488		

Table 1 *continued*

	January	February	March	April	May	June
II. Cash Gain or Loss for Month						
Collections	$ 89 140	X	X	X	X	X
Payments:						
Purchases	X	X	X	X	X	$ 9 488
Labour						
2 months prior to sale	21 000					6 600
1 month prior to sale	42 000	49 000	56 000	44 800	29 400	19 600
General/administrative expenses	22 000	X	X	X	X	X
Lease	7 500	X	X	X	X	X
Miscellaneous expenses	6 750	X	X	X	X	X
Taxes			18 000			18 000
Interest (on bonds)	15 000					
New equipment						125 000
Total payments	$138 438	X	X	X	X	X
Net cash gain (loss)	($ 49 298)	($19 138)	X	X	X	X
III. Cash Surplus or Loan Requirements						
Cash at start if no borrowing is done	$ 70 000	$20 703	X	X	X	X
Cumulative cash	$ 20 703	X	X	X	X	X
Target cash balance	70 000	X	X	X	X	X
Surplus cash or total loans outstanding to maintain target cash balance	($ 49 298)	X	X	X	X	X

Table 2
Daily Cash Budget Worksheet

				Day											
	1	2	***	5	***	10	11	***	14	15	***	28	29	30	31
I. Collections and Payments															
Gross sales	$ 3 871	X	***	$ 3 871	***	$3 871	$3 871	***	$3 871	$3 871	***	X	X	$3 871	$3 871
Collections:															
Discount payers	$ 427	X		X		X	$ 569		X	$ 569		X	X	$ 569	$ 569
Net payers	1 887	X		X		X	1 887		X	1 887		X	X	1 887	2 516
Late payers	433	X		X		X	433		X	433		X	X	433	581
Total collections	$ 2 747	$2 747	***	$ 2 747	***	$2 747	$2 889	***	$2 889	$2 889	***	$2 889	$2 889	$2 889	$3 666
Purchases	$26 250														
Payments:															
2 months prior to sale				X											
1 month prior to sale				$12 375											
Total payments	$ 0	$ 0	***	$24 188	***	$ 0	$ 0	***	$ 0	$ 0	***	$ 0	$ 0	$ 0	$ 0

Table 2 *continued*

	Day														
	1	2	***	5	***	10	11	***	14	15	***	28	29	30	31
II. Cash Gain or Loss for day															
Collections	$ 2 747	$ 2 747	***	$ 2 747	***	X	X	***	$2 889	$ 2 889	***	$ 2 889	$2 889	$2 889	$3 666
Payments:															
Purchases				$24 188											
Labour															
2 months before sale	$10 500									$10 500					
1 month before sale	21 000									21 000					
General/administrative expenses	11 000									11 000					
Lease	X														
Miscellaneous expenses	218			218		218	218		218	218		218	218	218	218
Taxes		X								15 000					
Interest (on bonds)															
Total payments	$50 218	$ 218	***	$24 405	***	$ 218	$218	***	$ 218	$57 718	***	$ 218	$ 218	$ 218	$ 218
Net cash gain (loss)	($47 471)	($ X)	***	($21 658)	***	$2 529	$2 672	***	$2 672	($54 828)	***	$2 672	$2 672	$2 672	$3 448

Table 2 *continued*

											Day				
	1	2	***	5	***	10	11	***	14	15	***	28	29	30	31
III. Cash Surplus or Loan Requirements															
Cash at start if no borrowing is done	$70 000	$22 529	***	$30 118	***	$18 578	$21 107	***	$29 122	$31 794	***	$ 9 026	X	$14 370	$17 042
Cumulative cash	$22 529	$25 059		$ 8 460		$21 107	$23 779		X	($23 034)		X	X	$17 042	$20 490
Target cash balance	70 000	70 000		70 000		70 000	70 000		X	70 000		X	X	70 000	70 000
Surplus cash or total loans outstanding to maintain target cash balance	($47 471)	($44 941)	***	($61 540)	***	($48 893)	($46 221)	***	X	($93 034)	***	($58 302)	($55 630)	($52 958)	($49 510)

19

Credit Policy

Kiddyland Clothes, Inc.

Kiddyland Clothes manufactures children's clothing, including such accessories as socks and belts. The company has been in business since 1952, mainly supplying private-label merchandise to large department stores. In 1987, however, the company started producing its own line of children's clothing under the brand name "Yuppiewear." An increasing number of two- income families has been accompanied by an increasing demand for high-status children's clothing, and Kiddyland was the first in its field to recognize this trend.

When Kiddyland's sales were primarily for private labels, the firm's financial manager did not have to worry much about its overall credit policy. Most of its sales were negotiated directly with the department stores' buyers, and the resulting contracts contained specific credit terms. The new line, however, represented a significant change—it is sold through numerous wholesalers under standard credit terms, so credit policy per se has become important. Vicki Leung, the assistant treasurer, has been assigned the task of reviewing the company's current credit policy and recommending any desirable changes.

Kiddyland's current credit terms are 2/10, net 30. Thus, wholesalers buying from Kiddyland receive a 2 percent discount off the gross purchase price if they pay within 10 days, while customers who do not take the discount must pay the full amount within 30 days. The company does check the financial strength of potential customers, but its standards for granting credit are not high. Similarly, it does have procedures for collecting past-due accounts, but its collections policy could best be described as passive. Gross sales to wholesalers average about $10 million a year, and 50 percent of the paying wholesalers (by dollar volume) take the discount and pay, on average, on Day 10. Another 30 percent of the payers generally pay the full amount on Day 30, while 20 percent tend to stretch Kiddyland's terms and do not actually pay, on average, until Day 40. Two percent of Kiddyland's gross sales to wholesalers end up as bad debt losses.

Geoff Reiner, the treasurer and Vicki Leung's boss, is convinced that the firm should tighten its credit policy. According to Reiner, good customers will pay on time regardless of the terms, and the ones who would complain about a tighter policy are probably not good customers. Vicki must make an analysis and then recommend a course of action. For political reasons, she has decided to focus on a tighter policy, under which a 4 percent discount would be offered to customers who pay cash on delivery (COD), and 20 days of credit would be offered to customers who elect not to take the discount. Also, under the new policy, stricter credit standards would be applied, and a tougher collection policy would be enforced. This policy has been dubbed "4/COD, net 20."

Geoff Reiner likes this policy—he believes that increasing the discount would both bring in new customers and encourage more of Kiddyland's existing customers to take the discount. As a result, he believes that sales to wholesalers would increase from $10 million to $11 million annually, that 60 percent of the paying customers would take the discount, that 30 percent of the payers would pay on Day 20, that 10 percent would pay late on Day 30, and that bad-debt losses would be reduced to 1 percent of gross sales. Reiner's is not the only position, though—Bob Silva, the sales manager, has argued for an easier credit policy. Silva thinks that the proposed change would result in a drastic loss of sales and profits.

Kiddyland's variable cost-to-sales ratio is 75 percent; its pre-tax cost of carrying receivables is 12 percent; and the company can expand without any problems (or any cost increases) because it can subcontract production that it cannot handle in house. Further, Geoff Reiner is convinced that neither the variable cost ratio nor the cost of capital would change as a result of a credit policy change. Bob Silva, however, thinks that the variable cost ratio might increase significantly if sales rise so much that the company is forced to use outside suppliers. Also, Silva, based on discussions with the cost accounting staff, thinks that the variable cost ratio might rise as high as 90 percent this coming year, even without an increase in sales, due to higher labour costs under a contract now being negotiated. Everyone agrees that there is little chance that costs will decline, regardless of the credit policy decision. Kiddyland's federal-plus-provincial tax rate is 40 percent.

Now Vicki Leung must conduct an analysis to estimate the effect of the proposed credit policy change on Kiddyland's profitability. She and Geoff Reiner are very much concerned about the analysis, both because of its importance to the company and also because of its political implications—the sales and production people have been lobbying against any credit tightening because they do not want to take a chance on losing sales and having to cut production, and also because they question the assumptions Reiner wants to use. Therefore, Leung knows that her report will be critically reviewed. Working with Reiner, she prepared the following set of questions for use as a guide in drafting her report. Put yourself in Vicki's position and then answer the following questions. As you answer each question, think about the follow-up questions that other people, such as those in sales and production, might ask when the report is being reviewed.

Questions

1. What are the four variables that make up a firm's credit policy? How likely (and how quickly) are competitors to respond to a change in each variable, and is their response likely to be the same for a change toward tightness as one toward looseness?

2. What is Kiddyland's current days sales outstanding (DSO) (also called average collection period [ACP])? What would be the expected DSO if the credit policy change were made?

3. What is the dollar amount of bad-debt losses under the current policy? What would be the expected bad-debt losses under the proposed policy?

4. What is the cost of granting discounts under the current policy? What would be the expected cost under the new policy?

5. What is Kiddyland's dollar cost of carrying receivables under the current policy? What would be the expected cost under the new policy? (Use a 360-day year.)

6. What is the expected incremental profit associated with the proposed change in credit terms? Should Kiddyland make the change? (Hint: Construct income statements under each policy, and focus on the expected change. See Table 1 for a guide.)

Table 1
Incremental Profit Analysis

	Proposed Policy	Current Policy	Difference
Gross sales	X	$10 000 000	X
Discounts taken	X	98 000	X
Net sales	X	$ 9 902 000	X
Production costs	X	7 500 000	X
Net earnings before credit costs	X	$ 2 402 000	X
Credit-related costs			
Receivables carrying cost	X	55 000	X
Bad-debt losses	X	200 000	X
Net earnings before taxes	X	$ 2 147 000	X
Taxes (40%)	X	858 800	X
After-tax profit	X	$ 1 288 200	X

7. Does your analysis up to this point consider the risks involved with a credit policy change? If not, how could risk be assessed and incorporated into the analysis?

8. Suppose the firm makes the change to 4/COD, net 20, but Kiddyland's competitors react by making similar changes in their terms. The net result is that Kiddyland's gross sales remain at the current $10 million level. If the remainder of Vicki's assumptions are correct, what would be the impact on Kiddyland's profitability?

9. Vicki expects both the sales and production managers to question her assumptions, so she would like to know which variables are most critical in the sense that profitability is very sensitive to them. Then, she would like to know just how far off her assumption could be before the change to a tighter credit policy would be incorrect. If you have access to the *Lotus* model, do some sensitivity analyses, changing one variable at a time while leaving the others at their base-case values. Which variables are most important in terms of their effects on profit, and how large an error could there be in the assumptions that you regard as being most critical before the decision should be reversed?

10. Also, if she could, Vicki Leung would like to have a better basis for the assumptions used in her report; as it stands, all she has to rely on is Geoff Reiner's judgement, which is contrary to that of two other senior executives. What are some actions that Vicki might take to improve the accuracy of her forecasts?

The following question presents an algebraic approach to analyzing changes in credit policy. Answer it only if it is assigned by your instructor.

11. As an alternative to constructing profit statements, an algebraic approach has been developed that focuses directly on the change in profits. To use this approach, it is first necessary to define the following symbols:

S_0 = current gross sales.

S_N = new gross sales after the change in credit policy. Note that S_N can be greater than or less than S_0.

V = variable costs as a percentage of gross sales. V includes production costs, inventory carrying costs, the cost of administering the credit department, and all other variable costs except bad-debt losses, receivables carrying costs, and the cost of giving discounts.

$1 - V$ = contribution margin, or the proportion of gross sales that goes toward covering fixed costs and increasing profits.

k = cost of financing the firm's receivables.

DSO_0 = current days sales outstanding

DSO_N = new average days sales outstanding after change in credit policy.

B_0 = current bad-debt losses as a proportion of current gross sales.

B_N = new bad-debt losses as a proportion of new gross sales.

P_0 = proportion of current-collected gross sales that are discount sales.

P_N = proportion of new-collected gross sales that are discount sales.

D_0 = current discount offered.

D_N = discount offered under new policy.

T = tax rate.

Calculate values for the incremental change in the firm's investment in receivables, ΔI, and the incremental change in after-tax profits, ΔP, as follows:

$$\Delta I = V[(DSO_N - DSO_0)(\frac{S_0}{360})] + V[(DSO_N)\frac{(S_N - S_0)}{360}].$$

$$\Delta P = (1-T)(S_N - S_0)(1 - V) - k\Delta I - (B_N S_N - B_0 S_0) - [(D_N S_N P_N(1 - B_N) - D_0 S_0 P_0(1 - B_0))].$$

Note that, in the profit equation, the first term, $(1 - T)(S_N - S_0)(1 - V)$, is the incremental gross profit, the second term, $k\Delta I$, is the incremental cost of carrying receivables, the third term, $B_N S_N - B_0 S_0$, is the incremental bad-debt losses, and the last term, $D_N S_N P_N(1 - B_N) - D_0 S_0 P_0(1 - B_0)$, is the incremental cost of discounts.[1]

Use the equations presented here to estimate the change in profits associated with the new policy.

---

1 Note that the analysis presented here is somewhat simplified in that the opportunity cost of the incremental investment in receivables from current customers is not considered. For a complete discussion of the analysis, see Eugene F. Brigham and Louis C. Gapenski, *Intermediate Financial Management*, 3rd ed., Chapter 19.

VIII

Financial Analysis and Forecasting

Case 20
Financial Analysis and Forecasting National Trailer Company (A)

Case 21
Financial Forecasting Real Estate Management Systems Company

20

*Financial
Analysis and
Forecasting*

National Trailer
Company (A)

National Trailer Company manufactures farm and specialty trailers of all types. More than 85 percent of the company's sales come from central Canada, although a growing market for custom livestock transport vans designed and produced by National is developing nationally and even internationally. Also, several major boat companies in Ontario and the Atlantic provinces have had National design and manufacture trailers for their new models, and these boat-trailer "packages" are sold through the boat companies' nationwide dealer networks.

Tim Hagerman, the founder and president of National, recently received a call from Karen Green, vice-president of the eastern Ontario region of the Traders Bank of Canada. Green told Hagerman that a deficiency report, generated by the bank's computerized analysis system, had been filed because of National's deteriorating financial position. The bank requires quarterly financial statements from each of its major loan customers. Information from such statements is fed into the computer, which then calculates key ratios for each customer and charts trends in these ratios. The system also compares the statistics for each company with the average ratios of other firms in the same industry and against any protective covenants in the loan agreements. If any ratio is significantly worse than the industry average, reflects a marked adverse trend, or fails to meet contractual requirements, the computer highlights the deficiency.

The latest deficiency report on National revealed a number of adverse trends, and several potentially serious problems (see Tables 1 through 6 for National's historical financial statements). Particularly disturbing were the 1990 current, quick, and debt ratios, all of which failed to meet the contractual limits of 2.0, 1.0, and 55 percent, respectively. Technically, the bank had a legal right to call all the loans it had extended to National for immediate repayment, and, if the loans were not repaid within 10 days, to force the company into bankruptcy.

Karen Green hoped to avoid calling the loans if at all possible, as she knew that this would back National into a corner from which it might not be able to emerge. Still, she knew that the bank's senior loan committee were very strict in their examination of bank loan portfolios and demanded early identification of potential repayment problems.

One measure of the quality of a loan is the Altman Z factor, which for National was 2.97 for 1990, just below the 2.99 minimum that is used to differentiate strong firms, which have little likelihood of bankruptcy in the next 2 years, from those deemed likely to go into default. This will put the bank under increased pressure to reclassify National's loans as "problem loans," to set up a reserve to cover potential losses, and to take whatever steps are necessary to reduce the bank's exposure. Setting up the loss reserve would have a negative effect on the bank's profits and reflect badly on Karen Green's performance.

To keep National's loan from being reclassified as a "problem loan," the senior loan committee will require strong and convincing evidence that the company's present difficulties are only temporary. Therefore, it must be shown that appropriate actions to overcome the problems have been taken and that the chances of reversing the adverse trends are realistically good. Karen Green now has the task of collecting the necessary information, evaluating its implications, and preparing a recommendation for action.

The recession that has plagued the Canadian farm economy since the early 1980s had caused severe, though probably temporary, problems for companies like National. On top of this, droughts for two straight summers had devastated the Prairie provinces' wheat crops, leading to a drastic curtailment of demand for new trailers and transport carriers. In light of the softening demand, National had aggressively reduced prices in 1989 and 1990 to stimulate sales. This, the company believed, would allow it to realize greater economies of scale in production and to ride the learning, or experience, curve down to a lower cost position. National's management had full confidence that national economic policies would revive the ailing farm sector, and that the downturn in demand would only be a short-term problem. Consequently, production continued unabated, and inventories increased sharply.

In a further effort to reduce inventory, National relaxed its credit standards in early 1990, and it improved its already favourable credit terms. As a result, sales growth did remain high by industry standards through the third quarter of 1990, but not high enough to keep inventories from continuing to rise. Further, the credit policy changes had caused accounts receivable to increase dramatically by late 1990.

To finance its rising inventories and receivables, National turned to the bank for a long-term loan in 1989, and it also increased its short-term credit

Table 1
Historical and Pro Forma Balance Sheets
for Years Ended December 31
(Thousands of Dollars)

	Historical			Pro Forma	
	1988	**1989**	**1990**	**1991**	**1992**
Assets					
Cash and marketable securities	$ 5 149	$ 4 004	$ 3 906	$ 37 339	X
Accounts receivable	17 098	18 462	X	18 442	20 194
Inventory	18 934	33 029	46 659	30 029	X
Current assets	$41 181	$55 495	$79 922	X	$101 466
Land, buildings, plant, and equipment	$17 761	$20 100	$22 874	$ 29 249	$ 30 126
Accumulated depreciation	(2 996)	(4 654)	(6 694)	(9 117)	(10 940)
Net fixed assets	$14 765	$15 446	$16 180	$ 20 132	$ 19 186
Total assets	$55 946	$70 941	$96 102	$105 942	X
Liabilities and Equity					
Short-term bank loans	$ 3 188	$ 5 100	$18 233	$24 608	X
Accounts payable	6 764	10 506	19 998	15 995	16 795
Accruals	3 443	5 100	7 331	9 301	11 626
Current liabilities	$13 395	$20 706	$45 562	X	X
Long-term bank loans	$ 6 375	$ 9 563	$ 9 563	9 563	9 563
Mortgage	2 869	2 601	2 340	2 104	1 894
Long-term debt	$ 9 244	$12 164	$11 903	$11 667	$11 457
Total liabilities	$22 639	$32 870	$57 465	X	X
Common stock	$23 269	$23 269	$23 269	$23 269	$23 269
Retained earnings	10 038	14 802	15 368	21 103	X
Total equity	$33 307	$38 071	X	$44 372	X
Total liabilities and equities	$55 946	$70 941	$96 102	X	X

Notes:
a. 3 500 000 shares of common stock were outstanding throughout the period 1988–1990.
b. Market price of shares: 1988—$17.79; 1989—$9.69; 1990—$3.74.
c. Price-earnings (P/E) ratios: 1988—6.61; 1989—5.35; 1990—17.0. The 1990 P/E ratio is high because of the depressed earnings that year.
d. Assume that all changes in interest-bearing loans and gross fixed assets occur at the start of the relevant years.
e. The mortgage loan is secured by a first-mortgage bond on land and buildings.

lines in both 1989 and 1990. However, this expanded credit was insufficient to cover the asset expansion, so the company began to delay payments of its accounts payable until the second late notice had been received. Management realized that this was not a particularly wise decision for the long run, but they did not think it would be necessary to follow the policy for very

Table 2
Historical and Pro Forma Income Statements
for Years Ended December 31
(Thousands of Dollars)

	Historical			Pro Forma	
	1988	1989	1990	1991	1992
Net sales	$170 998	$184 658	$195 732	$207 476	$227 186
Cost of goods sold	137 684	151 761	166 837	171 168	X
Gross profit	$ 33 314	$ 32 897	$ 28 895	$ 36 308	$ 45 437
Administrative and selling expenses	$ 12 790	$ 15 345	$ 16 881	$ 16 598	X
Depreciation	1 594	1 658	2 040	2 423	1 823
Miscellaneous expenses	2 027	3 557	5 725	X	2 840
Total operating expenses	$ 16 411	$ 20 560	X	X	X
EBIT	$ 16 903	$ 12 337	$ 4 249	$ 13 656	X
Interest on short-term loans	$ 319	$ 561	$ 1 823	$ 2 953	$ 2 953
Interest on long-term loans	638	956	956	956	956
Interest on mortgage	258	234	211	189	170
Total interest	$ 1 215	$ 1 751	$ 2 990	$ 4 098	$ 4 079
Before-tax earnings	$ 15 688	$ 10 586	$ 1 259	X	$ 19 656
Taxes	6 275	4 234	504	3 823	7 863
Net income	$ 9 413	$ 6 351	$ 755	X	X
Dividends on stock	2 353	1 588	189	0	X
Additions to retained earnings	$ 7 060	$ 4 764	$ 566	X	X

Notes:
a. Earnings per share (EPS): 1988—$2.69; 1989—$1.81; 1990—$0.22.
b. Interest rates on borrowed funds:
   Short-term loan: 1988—10%; 1989—11%; 1990—10%.
   Long-term loan: 10% for each year.
   Mortgage: 9% for each year.
c. For purposes of this case, assume that expenses other than depreciation and interest are all variable with sales.

long—the 1990 summer wheat crop looked like a record breaker, and it was unlikely that a severe drought would again destroy the crop. Also, the major boat companies were forecasting record-breaking sales for the coming years, so National was optimistic that its stable and profitable markets of the past would soon reappear.

After Karen Green's telephone call, and the subsequent receipt of a copy of the bank's financial analysis of National, Tim Hagerman began to realize just how precarious his company's financial position had become. As he started to reflect on what could be done to correct the problems, it suddenly

Table 3

Common Size Balance Sheets

for Years Ended December 31

(Amounts in Percentage of Total Assets)

	1988	1989	1990
Assets			
Cash and marketable securities	9.20	5.64	4.06
Accounts receivable	30.56	26.02	X
Inventory	33.84	46.56	48.55
Current assets	73.61	78.23	X
Land, buildings, plant, and equipment	31.75	28.33	X
Accumulated depreciation	(5.36)	(6.56)	(6.97)
Net fixed assets	26.39	21.77	16.84
Total assets	100.00	100.00	100.00
Liabilities and Equity			
Short-term bank loans	5.70	7.19	18.97
Accounts payable	12.09	14.81	20.81
Accruals	6.15	7.19	7.63
Current liabilities	23.94	29.19	47.41
Long-term bank loans	11.39	13.48	X
Mortgage	5.13	3.67	2.43
Long-term debt	16.52	17.15	X
Total liabilities	40.47	46.33	59.80
Common stock	41.59	32.80	24.21
Retained earnings	17.94	20.86	X
Total equity	59.53	53.66	40.20
Total liabilities and equities	100.00	100.00	100.00

dawned on him that the company was in even more trouble than the bank imagined. Hagerman had recently signed a contract for a plant expansion that would require an additional $6 375 000 of capital during the first quarter of 1991, and he had planned to obtain this money with a short-term loan from the bank to be repaid from profits expected in the last half of 1991 as a result of the expansion. In his view, once the new production facility went on line, the company would be able to increase output in several segments of the trailer market. It might have been possible to cut back on the expansion plans and to retrench, but because of the signed construction contracts and the cancellation charges that would be imposed if the plans were cancelled, Hagerman correctly regards the $6 375 000 of new capital as being essential for National's very survival.

Hagerman quickly called his senior management team in for a meeting, explained the situation, and asked for their help in formulating a solution. The group concluded that if the company's current business plan were

Table 4

Common-Size Income Statements

for Years Ended December 31

(Amounts in Percentage of Net Sales)

	1988	1989	1990
Net sales	100.00	100.00	100.00
Cost of goods sold	80.52	82.18	X
Gross profit	19.48	17.82	14.76
Administrative and selling expenses	7.48	8.31	8.62
Depreciation	0.93	0.90	X
Miscellaneous expenses	1.19	1.93	2.92
Total operating expenses	9.60	11.13	12.59
EBIT	9.88	6.68	2.17
Interest on short-term loans	0.19	0.30	X
Interest on long-term loans	0.37	0.52	X
Interest on mortgage	0.15	0.13	0.11
Total interest	0.71	0.95	1.53
Before-tax earnings	9.17	5.73	0.64
Taxes	3.67	2.29	X
Net income	5.50	3.44	0.39
Dividends on stock	1.38	0.86	0.10
Additions to retained earnings	4.13	2.58	0.29

carried out, National's sales would grow by 6 percent from 1990 to 1991, and by another 9.5 percent from 1991 to 1992. Further, they concluded that National should reverse its recent policy of aggressive pricing and easy credit, returning to pricing that fully covered costs plus normal profit margins and to standard industry credit practices. These changes should enable the company to reduce the cost of goods sold from over 85 percent of sales in 1990 to about 82.5 percent in 1991, and then to 80 percent in 1992. Similarly, the management group felt that the company could reduce administrative and selling expenses from almost 9 percent of sales in 1990 to 8 percent in 1991, and then to 7.5 percent in 1992. Significant cuts should also be possible in miscellaneous expenses, which should fall from 2.92 percent of 1990 sales to approximately 1.75 percent of sales in 1991, and to 1.25 percent in 1992. These cost reductions represented "trimming the fat," so they were not expected to influence the quality of the firm's products or its effective sales efforts. Further, to appease suppliers, future bills could be paid more promptly, and to convince the bank how serious management is about correcting the company's problems, cash dividends would be eliminated until the firm regains its financial health.

Assume that Tim Hagerman has hired you as a consultant to first verify the bank's evaluation of the company's current financial situation and then to put together a forecast of National's expected performance for 1991 and 1992. Hagerman asks you to develop some figures that ignore the possibility

Table 5

Statement of Cash Flows

for Years Ended December 31

(Thousands of Dollars)

	1989	1990
Cash Flow from Operations		
Sales	$184 658	$195 732
Increase in receivables	(1 364)	X
Cash sales	$183 294	$184 837
Cost of goods sold	($151 761)	($166 837)
Increase in inventories	(14 095)	(13 630)
Increase in accounts payable	3 742	9 492
Increase in accruals	1 657	X
Cash cost of goods	($160 457)	X
Cash margin	$ 22 837	X
Administrative and selling expenses	(15 345)	(16 881)
Miscellaneous expenses	(3 557)	(5 725)
Taxes	(4 234)	(504)
Net cash-flow from operations	($ 299)	X
Cash Flow from Fixed Asset Investment		
Investment in fixed assets	($ 2 339)	($ 2 774)
Cash Flow from Financing Activities		
Increase in short-term debt	1 912	13 133
Increase in long-term debt	3 188	X
Repayment of mortgage	(268)	(261)
Interest expense	(1 751)	(2 990)
Common dividends	(1 588)	(189)
Net cash flow from financial activities	$ 1 493	$ 9 693
Net increase (decrease) in cash and marketable securities	($ 1 145)	X

of a reduction in the credit lines and assume that the bank will increase the line of credit by the $6 375 000 needed for the expansion and supporting working capital. Also, you and Hagerman do not expect the level of interest rates to change substantially over the 2-year forecast period; however, you both think that the bank will charge 12 percent on both the additional short-term loan, if it is granted, and on the existing short-term loans, if they are extended. The assumed 40 percent combined federal and provincial tax rate should also hold for 2 years. Finally, if the bank co-operates, and if Hagerman is able to turn the company around, the price-to-earnings ratio should be 10 in 1991 but rise to 12 in 1992.

Your first task is to construct a set of pro forma financial statements that Hagerman and the rest of the National management team can use to assess the company's position and to convince Karen Green that her bank's loan is

Table 6
Historical and Pro Forma Ratio Analysis
for Years Ended December 31

	Historical			Pro Forma		Industry
	1988	**1989**	**1990**	**1991**	**1992**	Average[f]
Liquidity Ratios[a]						
Current ratio	3.07	2.68	X	X	X	2.50
Quick ratio	1.66	1.08	0.73	1.12	X	1.00
Leverage Ratios						
Debt ratio	40.47%	46.33%	X	X	53.45%	50.00%
Times-interest-earned ratio	13.92	7.04	1.42	X	5.82	7.70
Asset Management Ratios						
Inventory turnover (cost)[b]	7.27	4.59	3.58	5.70	5.70	5.70
Inventory turnover (selling)[c]	9.03	5.59	4.19	X	X	7.00
Fixed assets turnover	11.58	11.96	12.10	10.31	11.84	12.00
Total assets turnover	3.06	2.60	2.04	1.96	X	3.00
Days sales outstanding[d]	36.00	35.99	X	X	32.00	32.00
Profitability Ratios						
Profit margin	5.50%	3.44%	0.39%	X	X	2.90%
Gross profit margin	19.48%	17.82%	14.76%	17.50%	20.00%	18.00%
Return on total assets	16.83%	8.95%	X	5.41%	9.78%	8.80%
Return on owner equity	28.26%	16.68%	1.95%	X	X	17.50%
Potential Failure Indicator						
Altman Z factor[e]	6.55	4.68	2.97	3.63	X	4.65
Dividend payout ratio	25.00%	25.00%	25.00%	0.00%	X	20.00%

Notes:
[a]Year-end balance sheet values were used throughout in the computation of ratios embodying   balance sheet items.
[b]Uses cost of goods sold as the numerator.
[c]Uses net sales as the numerator.
[d]Assume year has 360 days.
[e]Altman's function is calculated as

$$Z = 0.012X_1 + 0.014X_2 + 0.033X_3 + 0.006X_4 + 0.999X_5 \,.$$

Here
X_1 = net working capital/total assets.
X_2 = retained earnings/total assets.
X_3 = EBIT/total assets.
X_4 = market value of common and preferred stock/book value of debt.
X_5 = sales/total assets.
The "Altman Z factor" range of 1.81–2.99 represents the so-called "zone of ignorance." Refer to Chapter 20 of Eugene F. Brigham and Louis C. Gapenski, *Intermediate Financial Management*, (Hinsdale, Ill: Dryden Press, 1990), for details concerning the Z factor.
[f]Assume constant industry-average ratios throughout the period 1988–1992.

safe, provided the bank will extend the National's line of credit. Then, you must present your projections, with recommendations for future action, to National's management and to Karen Green. To prepare for your presentations, answer the following questions, keeping in mind that both the National managers and, particularly, Karen Green and possibly her bosses, could ask you some tough questions about your analysis and recommendations. Put another way, the following questions are designed to help you focus on the issues, but they are not meant to be a complete and exhaustive list of all the relevant points.

Questions

1. Complete the 1990 columns of Tables 1 through 6, disregarding for now the projected data in the 1991 and 1992 columns. To be consistent with the financial community, assume that a year has 360 days. If you have access to the *Lotus* model, use it to complete the tables. Be sure you understand all the numbers, as it would be most embarrassing (and fatal to your career as a consultant) if you were asked how you got a particular number and you could not give a meaningful response.

2. Based on the information in the case and on the results of your calculations in Question 1, prepare a list of National's strengths and weaknesses. In essence, you should look at the common-size statements and each key ratio and see what they indicate about the company's operations. Use the extended Du Pont system to highlight the key relationships as a part of your answer.

3. Recognizing that you might want to revise your opinion later, does it appear, based on your analysis to this point, that the bank should be willing to lend the requested money to National? Explain.

4. Now complete the tables to develop pro forma financial statements for 1991 and 1992. For these calculations, assume that the bank is willing to maintain the present credit lines and to grant an additional $6 375 000 of short-term credit effective January 1, 1991. In the analysis, take account of the amounts of inventory and accounts receivable that would be carried if inventory utilization (based on the cost of goods sold) and the days sales outstanding (average collection period) were set at industry-average levels. Also, assume in your forecast that all of National's plans and predictions concerning sales and expenses materialize, and that National pays no cash dividends during the forecast period. Finally, in your calculations, use the cash and marketable securities account as the residual balancing figure. Complete the *Lotus* model if you have access to it.

5. Assume that National has determined that its optimal cash balance is 5 percent of sales, and that funds in excess of this amount will be invested in marketable securities that, on average, will earn 7 percent interest. Based on your forecasted financial statements, will National be able to invest in marketable securities in 1991 and 1992? Do your financial forecasts reveal any developing conditions that should be corrected?

6. Based on the forecasts developed earlier, would National be able to retire all of the outstanding short-term loans by December 31, 1991? In answering this question, assume that National will, if possible, repay the loans at a constant rate throughout the year. Therefore, on average, the amount of short-term loans outstanding will be half of the beginning-of-year amount.

7. If the bank decides to withdraw the entire line of credit and to demand immediate repayment of the two existing loans, what alternatives would be available to National?

8. Under what circumstances might the validity of any comparative ratio analysis be questionable? Answer this question in general terms, not just in terms of National, but use National data to illustrate your points.

9. Revise your pro forma financial statements for 1991 and 1992, assuming both of the following conditions:
   (1) Short-term loans will be repaid when sufficient cash is available to do so without reducing the liquidity of the firm below the minimum requirements set by the bank, and when the company is able to maintain at least the minimum cash balance (5 percent).
   (2) National will reinstate a 25 percent cash dividend in the year that all short-term loans and credit lines have been paid in full.

10. On the basis of your analyses, do you think that Karen Green should recommend that the bank extend the existing short- and long-term loans, and grant the additional $6 375 000 loan, or that the bank demand immediate repayment of all existing loans? If she does recommend continuing to support the company, what conditions (for example, collateral, guarantees, or other safeguards) might the bank impose to protect itself? Explain.

11. It is apparent that National's future, and that of the bank loan, is critically dependent on the company's operating conditions in 1991 and 1992. The assumptions used produce good results, but actual results could be disastrous. Because of this, it would be useful if you could, as part of your consulting report, inform management—and the bank—as to how sensitive the results are to such things as the sales growth rate, the cost of goods sold percentage, the administrative expense ratio. If the results would still look fairly good, even if those factors were not as favourable as forecasted, the bank would have greater confidence in extending the

requested credit. On the other hand, if even tiny changes in these variables would lead to a continuation of the past downward trend, the bank would still be leery. If you have access to the *Lotus 1-2-3* model, do some sensitivity analyses (using data tables) to shed light on this issue. If you do not have access to the model, describe how one would go about a sensitivity (or scenario) analysis, but do not quantify your answer.

21

Financial
Forecasting

Real Estate Management Systems Company

Real Estate Management Systems Company (REMSCO) was founded in 1982 by two professors—one in real estate and one in computer science—to develop a new computer system for analyzing and managing commercial real estate. The plan was to develop a complex, integrated *Lotus 1-2-3* model that would be built into a customized computer chip and then be permanently installed in an IBM PC clone. Further, they planned to keep up with developments in both the real estate and computer industries, and to offer periodic updates that would enable their customers to deal efficiently with tax and regulatory changes.

REMSCO was successful from the start, and by 1990 it was an industry leader and growing rapidly. Colin MacNeil, who had been brought in as financial manager, had developed a good initial financial plan, and everything had gone smoothly. MacNeil knew, though, that the company had been lucky, and that some large real estate companies, including Coldwell Banker, were thinking about marketing a competitive system. Also, a rumour was going around that Lotus Development Corporation was thinking of developing a competitive product. REMSCO had not been sitting idle—the company now markets a PC-based personal tax preparation package that sells well, and other products are also in the pipeline. Further, REMSCO's real estate customers are quite satisfied, and word-of-mouth promotion has become one of the company's most important assets. Finally, it would be costly for its real estate customers to change systems, so they will probably keep buying REMSCO's add-ons and modified systems unless some competitor develops a truly outstanding new product.

REMSCO's financial planning process is broken down into five steps:

(1) A study is made of basic trends in the computer industry, and also in the real estate and other markets where REMSCO expects to operate. Questions such as these are addressed: Our basic real estate analysis

program is based on *Lotus* Release 2; should we go to Release 3? How will our customers' needs change over the next 5 years, and what can we do to meet any existing or developing needs?

(2) A set of pro forma financial statements is developed and used to analyze the effects of alternative operating plans on projected profits and financial ratios. The plan encompasses 5 years, with the projections being relatively detailed for the coming year and much less detailed for the following 4 years. The entire plan is updated every year, in November.

(3) The specific financial requirements needed to support the company's base-case operating plan are determined. This information is obtained from the pro forma statements.

(4) The specific sources of capital that will be used to meet the financial requirements are identified.

(5) The initially projected financial statements are then modified to include the addition of the capital needed to finance the projected assets. This involves adjusting the pro forma income statement to include the interest charges associated with any additional debt, and an adjustment to dividends paid if new stock must be issued. These modifications change the initially projected retained earnings, and thus change the "additional funds needed" to finance the asset expansion. These feedback effects require the use of an iterative process to produce a consistent final set of financial statements. In the past, all this has been done manually, which takes a good bit of time, but MacNeil has been working to develop a computerized model to speed up the process.

REMSCO's 1989 and 1990 historical financial statements, along with a partially completed worksheet for use in forecasting, are given in Tables 1 and 2. The company was operating its fixed assets at full capacity in 1990, so its $30 297 240 of sales represented full capacity sales. Since the firm's marketing department is forecasting a 20 percent increase in sales for 1991, new assets will have to be added. For planning purposes, MacNeil assumes (1) that accounts payable and accruals will grow spontaneously in accordance with standard industry practices, (2) that new long-term capital will be raised in accordance with the firm's target capitalization ratios, which call for 20 percent long-term debt and 80 percent common equity (measured at market value), and (3) that short-term bank loans, reported as notes payable, will be used only to finance temporary working capital needs.

REMSCO currently has 5 million shares of common stock outstanding, and the market price is $6 per share. The dividend in 1990 was $0.20 per share, and management does not intend to increase the dividend in 1991. New long- term debt would carry a 12.0 percent coupon, and it would be issued at par.

REMSCO's senior managers go off on a one week retreat each November to work on the 5-year plan and the budget for the coming year. Prior to the retreat, the various division managers must prepare reports, which the top executives will review beforehand and then discuss at the retreat. As financial manager, Colin MacNeil normally prepares some first approximation financial forecasts, which are then modified during the retreat as a result of strategic decisions made at that time. The modified statements are used to show the financial implications of different operating plans. However, MacNeil recently underwent a difficult ulcer operation, and due to a slow recovery, he will not be able to attend the retreat, or to prepare the background report for it. Therefore his assistant, ready or not, must assume his duties.

MacNeil told the assistant that he had almost finished a computerized model that would aid in the process. MacNeil also indicated that the model needed to be debugged, or at least checked out, by first making a "by-hand" projection and then seeing if the model generated the same set of data. If a discrepancy is discovered, it will be necessary to find out where the error lies. MacNeil also cautioned his assistant that it might be necessary to explain to the executives how any changes in operating conditions would affect the funds requirements, and also how any changes in the financing mix would affect *everything*, including the funds requirements, the earnings per share, and the stock price. In particular, MacNeil warned the assistant not to try to defend the inputs to the forecasting process; rather, the critical thing is to be able to make adjustments in the likely event that the senior executives won't like all the assumptions used in the forecast. As MacNeil pointed out, "It's the top managers' job to understand the business and to make the final assumptions used in the forecast and the budget. It's our job to tell them how those assumptions interact, and what the final outcome will be if their assumptions hold true. We ought to use reasonable inputs for our report and basic forecasts, but our real job in the planning process is to show top management what will happen under different operating conditions."

Assume that you are MacNeil's assistant, and that you must take his place at the retreat. Prepare for the event by answering the following questions, and also consider any additional questions that you might be asked at the retreat.

Questions

1. Use the percentage-of-sales method to prepare REMSCO's 1991 pro forma financial statements. Assume that the asset account balances for 1990 are optimal for that year's sales. Proceed by completing the 1st Pass columns in Tables 1 and 2. Explain why total assets and total-liabilities-plus-equity are not equal, why it is necessary to go through a series of iterations, and why a balanced solution is eventually reached. (If you

have access to the *Lotus* model, you can use your Table 1 and Table 2 data later to check to see if you completed the model correctly.)

2. What mix of long-term debt and equity should the firm use to finance the shortfall? (Hint: The firm will finance with 20 percent debt and 80 percent equity, but retained earnings will take care of part of the equity requirements. Thus, the percentages must be applied to the total amount of new financing, including both retained earnings and the additional funds needed.)

3. Now complete the 2nd Pass columns of Tables 1 and 2 to develop the pro forma income statements and balance sheets that reflect financing feedback effects. (Hint: New long-term debt and common stock financing will increase REMSCO's interest expense and dividend payments, and hence reduce the first approximation addition to retained earnings.) Then go on to complete the 3rd Pass columns. Does a shortfall still exist after 3 passes? Explain.

4. Assume that you are now at the retreat, discussing the forecast with REMSCO's senior executives. The vice-president for manufacturing informs you that fixed assets were actually being operated at only 80 percent of capacity in 1990. What effect would this have on your projected external capital requirement for 1991? In answering this question, disregard any financing feedback effects, and answer the question by modifying the 1st Pass columns of Tables 1 and 2, but explain how you could go on to reach a balanced solution. Also, in answering this and the next question, assume that depreciation expenses remain constant as a percentage of sales.

5. In the 80-percent-of-capacity-utilization scenario, excess funds will be generated. Suppose one of the senior executives asked you, as the finance representative, what you would recommend doing with the money. How would you answer?

6. Rework Question 4 under the assumption that the firm was operating at 90 percent of capacity in 1990, and then discuss the general relationship between capacity utilization and projected capital requirements in situations (a) where assets are lumpy and (b) where they are not lumpy. (If you have access to the *Lotus 1-2-3* model, you could set up a data table and then graph the relationship between AFN and initial capacity utilization, in which the AFN figure reflects full financing feedback effects. Extensive modifications would be necessary to deal with lumpy assets.)

7. In general, what impact does a firm's dividend policy, profitability, and capital intensity have on its financing requirements? In this specific case, how do these factors affect REMSCO's financial requirements? (Again, if you have access to the *Lotus* model, you could do a sensitivity analysis

in which you change the capitalization ratios and the dividends, and then observe the effect on AFN. It would also be relatively easy to change the input data section to use a payout ratio rather than dividends per share in the event that management wanted to see the relationship between the payout and AFN. To change the profit margin, it would be necessary to change some of the ratios as given in Column 3 of the income statement shown in Table 1. This would, of course, depart from the assumption that the 1991 ratios will be the same as 1990 ratios.)

8. The percentage-of-sales method has been used to forecast the firm's financial statements. Suppose one of the senior executives asked you what assumptions are implied when one uses the percentage-of-sales method; that is, under what circumstances would the percentage-of-sales method produce a valid as opposed to an invalid forecast? How would you answer?

9. What are some other methods that could be used to forecast the asset and liability balances, and thus the forecasted financial requirements? If the senior executives asked you to incorporate these procedures into your analysis, how would you do it, how long would it take, and what additional data would you require?

10. The case states that REMSCO's optimal capital structure calls for 20 percent long-term debt and 80 percent common equity. However, according to the 1990 balance sheet, the firm's long-term-debt-to-capitalization ratio is long-term debt/total permanent capital = $5 600 000/($5 600 000 + $8 717 610) = 0.407 = 40.7%, and its total-debt-to-total-assets ratio is $7 115 370/$15 832 980 = 44.9%. Do these figures indicate that the capital structure is seriously out of balance, that the company is using far too much debt, and that you should modify the mix of debt and equity used in its forecasts? (Hint: Think about whether the optimal capital structure should be stated in book value or market value terms.)

11. Regardless of whether or not you think the capital structure *should* be changed, if it were changed, how would a change affect the other elements in the forecast, including the interest rate, the stock price, and the projected earnings per share? If you have access to the *Lotus* model, quantify your answer.

12. Calculate the following values based on the 1990 financial statements: (a) current ratio, (b) profit margin, (c) ROE, (d) book value per share, (e) EPS, (f) market/book ratio, and (g) P/E ratio. Then calculate those values for which you have the necessary data based on the base-case 1991 projected financial statements, and discuss how the projected ratios would change as such things as the sales growth rate, the payout ratio,

the capital structure, and the profit margin changed. Do you think the senior executives at the retreat would be interested in this type of data? If so, could you provide them with it on a "real-time" basis? Explain.

Table 1
Historical (1989 and 1990) and Projected Income Statements
(Thousands of Dollars)

	Actual		Percent-age of Sales	1st Pass 1991 (No Feed-backs)	2nd Pass 1991 (With Feed-backs)	3rd Pass 1991 (With Feed-backs)
	1989	1990				
Sales	$26 774.91	$30 297.24	100.00%			
Cost of goods sold	19 342.45	21 842.24	72.09			
Gross profit	$ 7 432.46	$ 8 455.00	27.91%			
Selling/admini-strative expenses	1 338.75	1 514.86	5.00			
Fixed operating costs	1 422.86	1 674.18	5.53			
Depreciation	782.19	734.22	2.42			
Miscellaneous expenses	300.44	342.94	1.13			
EBIT	$ 3 588.22	$ 4 188.80	13.83%			
Interest expense	276.00	261.00	n.s.[a]			
EBT	$ 3 312.22	$ 3 927.80	n.s.[a]			
Taxes	1 324.89	1 571.12	n.s.[a]			
Net income	$ 1 987.33	$ 2 356.68	n.s.[a]			
Dividends						
Addition to retained earnings						

Note: First complete the 1st Pass column; then go to Table 2 and complete the 1st Pass column; then use the information in Table 2 as inputs to complete the 2nd Pass column in Table 1. Continue on and complete the 3rd Pass column. You should find that the financing feedbacks lead to a greater need for external funds than was initially projected, but that these effects diminish rapidly in successive passes.
[a]n.s. = not spontaneous

Table 2
Historical (1989 and 1990) and Pro Forma Balance Sheets
(Thousands of Dollars)

	Actual		Percent-age of Sales	1st Pass 1991	2nd Pass 1991	3rd Pass 1991
	1989	1990				
Cash	$ 1 166.39	$ 1 788.58	5.90%			
Accounts receivable	4 462.49	5 049.54	16.67			
Inventories	4 549.14	4 776.59	15.77			
Current assets	$10 178.02	$11 614.71	38.34%			
Net fixed assets	3 818.95	4 218.27	13.92			
Total assets	$13 996.97	$15 832.98	52.26%			
Accounts payable	$ 1 027.40	$ 1 177.22	3.89%			
Accruals	208.64	238.15	0.79			
Notes payable	400.00	100.00	n.s.[a]			
Current liabilities	$ 1 636.04	$ 1 515.37	4.67%			
Long-term debt	5 000.00	5 600.00	n.s.[a]			
Total liabilities	$ 6 636.04	$ 7 115.37	n.s.[a]			
Common stock	$ 1 000.00	$ 1 000.00	n.s.[a]			
Retained earnings	6 360.93	7 717.61	n.s.[a]			
Total equity	$ 7 360.93	$ 8 717.61	n.s.[a]			
Liabilities + equity	$13 996.97	$15 832.98	n.s.[a]			

External capital needed
Projected new internal capital (retained earnings)
Projected total new capital
Raised this pass by selling debt (20%)
Raised this pass by selling stock (80% − retained earnings)
Total external capital
Additional interest expense this pass
Number of shares issued
Additional dividend payments this pass

Note: First fill in the 1st Pass column for Table 1, then the 1st Pass column for Table 2. You must allocate the funds shortfall between debt and equity, and then raise additional debt and/or equity. This additional capital will have effects on the 1st Pass income statement, which should be reflected in the 2nd Pass income statement. After 3 passes, the statements should be almost in balance. You could continue getting closer and closer approximations in additional passes, but three passes are sufficient in view of (1) the nature of the data and (2) the fact that *Lotus* models will produce an exact solution quite rapidly.
[a]n.s. = not spontaneous

IX

Bankruptcy and Mergers

Case 22
Bankruptcy and Reorganization National Trailer Company (B)

Case 23
Merger Analysis Handyware, Inc.

22

National Trailer Company (B)

National Trailer Company is in a precarious financial position—it is overextended, and unless the company can persuade its bank to continue present loans and also grant substantial additional credit, National may well go under. (At this point, see Part A of the case, and read the paragraphs preceding the questions to obtain background material necessary for working Part B. Also, the data for 1988, 1989, and 1990, as contained in Tables 1 and 2 in Part A, are necessary to work Part B.)

Before the bank can reach a decision on continuing support for National, Karen Green, the banker handling the National account, must prepare a report for the bank's senior loan committee. The report must contain a complete bankruptcy analysis setting forth the bank's exposure in the event of liquidation. To begin her analysis, Green estimated what values the assets would have if National were liquidated. Working with the bank's appraisers and liquidation experts, she concluded that the land and buildings could be sold for $5 million, while the equipment would bring in another $3 million. The receivables could be sold for $0.065 on the dollar, but the inventory would bring only $0.50 on the dollar.

Next, Green had to make sure that she understood the nature of the claims against National. The accruals currently (i.e., at the end of 1990) consist of $6 581 000 of sales and payroll taxes and $750 000 of accrued wages. The wages were all earned within the past 2 weeks, and no single employee is due more than $500. Long-term bank loans actually consist of two different loans: $5 million in straight unsecured debt, plus another $4 563 000 in loans that are subordinate to the $5 million loan. Green's employer, The Traders Bank, extended both the short-term loan and the senior long-term loan, while a competitor bank holds the subordinated note for $4 563 000. Green estimates that the administrative expenses for the trustee in bankruptcy would total $500 000—this amount would be "taken off the top" in any liquidation or reorganization procedure.

Now assume that you are Karen Green's assistant, and she has asked you to determine what would happen if the bank called its loans and forced National to be either reorganized or liquidated. Your job is to ascertain how the bank would fare in this event. You will have to make a report to Green, and perhaps also to the senior loan committee, so you should be able to answer any questions likely to be thrown at you. To get you started, you and Karen drew up a list of issues and set them forth in the following questions.

Questions

1. What are the differences between an informal and a formal bankruptcy proceeding, and between a reorganization and a liquidation? Also, explain the meaning of the terms "composition" and "extension" as they are used in bankruptcy proceedings. Could an agreement include both a composition and an extension?

2. What are the standards of "fairness" and "feasibility" as the terms are used in formal bankruptcy reorganizations?

3. What total dollar amount of funds could be expected, before any payments were made, if National were liquidated? Use Table 1 or the *Lotus* model in answering this question.

4. Develop a table showing the distribution of the expected proceeds to the "secured and preferred claimants," that is, those claimants who have precedence over the unsecured creditors. What dollar amount of proceeds would remain after the secured and preferred claimants had been paid? (Hint: Complete the top part of Table 1.)

5. Now create a table showing the distribution to unsecured creditors both before and after the adjustment for subordination. (Hint: Complete the remainder of Table 1.) What is the percentage of each claim (for both senior creditors and unsecured creditors) that would be paid in the final distribution? What would the stockholders get?

6. How would the Traders Bank and its competitor bank fare if National Trailer were liquidated, and what, in general terms, is the value to the Traders Bank of the subordination clause in the $4 563 000 long-term loan? What would be the impact on the Traders Bank if there were no subordination clause?

7. Now consider how the different creditors (and the stockholders) would fare under different assumptions about the amount of the liquidation proceeds. For example, what would the distribution to creditors be if the land and buildings brought only $2 million, or if they brought $8 mil-

lion? Similarly, how would the value received from the equipment, or the inventory, affect the distributions? If you are using the *Lotus* model, quantify your answer; otherwise, just discuss what would happen.

(If you were not assigned National Trailer Company (A), just discuss, in general terms, what is involved in Questions 8 and 9. If you are familiar with the National Trailer Company (A) case, answer the questions in more detail.)

8. If the assumptions that were used in Part A of the case were used here, in Part B, all of the creditors could be paid off, and the company would earn substantial profits, which would give value to the common stock. How should this situation affect the bank's decision as to whether or not to demand repayment of the loan? If the bank did demand repayment, how would the fact that the distributions depend so heavily on the assumptions used in the forecasts affect the Bankruptcy Court's decision to have the company reorganize versus liquidate? Put another way, do you suppose the Court would want to see operating projections based on different sets of assumptions, and some evidence as to which of the different sets of assumptions was most likely to be correct? Could probability distributions be used in this regard? Would a financial analyst working for the secured creditors be more likely to use a relatively optimistic set of assumptions? What if he or she worked for the common stockholders? Explain?

9. State whether or not you would recommend that the Court order a liquidation or a reorganization under each of the following scenarios: (1) You feel that the projections in Part A, where the projected profits are over $5 million per year, represent the most likely situation, and that there is almost no chance that the assets' liquidating value will decline. (2) You regard a second scenario, where annual profits are about $100 000, as most likely, but you also think there is a fairly high probability of either very good or very bad results. In the event of a bad outcome, the liquidating value of the assets will fall quickly and sharply from the current level. (3) You regard a third scenario, where annual profits are about –$1.5 million, as being most likely, but you also think there is about a 25 percent probability that the company's optimistic forecast would prove correct. Justify your choices, keeping in mind bankruptcy theory and law.

10. Based on all the information at hand, should Karen Green recommend that the bank force National into bankruptcy or lend it the necessary funds to keep going? Explain.

Table 1
Selected Case Data
(Thousands of Dollars)

Liquidation Proceeds

Cash and marketable securities	$ 3 906
Accounts receivable	19 082
Inventory	X
Land and buildings	5 000
Equipment	X
Total proceeds	$54 318

Distribution of Proceeds

Secured and Preferred Claims:

	Claim	Payment	Percentage of Claim Received	Proceeds Remaining after Claim is Paid
1. Mortgage	$2 340	$2 340	100.0%	$51 978
2. Trustee's fees	500	500	100.0	51 478
3. Wages due	X	X	X	X
4. Taxes due	5 000	5 000	100.0	44 147

Initial Unsecured Creditor Allocation:

Unsecured creditor claims	$47 794			
Proceeds remaining	$44 147			
Pro rata percentage	92.4%			
5. Accounts payable	$19 998	$18 472	92.4%	$25 675
6. Short-term bank loans	X	X	X	X
7. Priority long-term bank loans	5 000	4 618	92.4%	4 215
8. Subordinate long-term bank loans	4 563	4 215	92.4%	0
9. Remaining mortgage	0	0	N.A.	0

Unsecured Creditor Allocation after Subordination Adjustment:

10. Accounts payable	$19 998	$18 472	92.4%	$25 675
11. Short-term bank loans	18 233	16 842	92.4%	8 833
12. Priority long-term bank loans	5 000	5 000	100.0%	3 833
13. Subordinate long-term bank loans	X	4 215	X	X
14. Remaining mortgage	0	0	N.A.	0

Shareholders' Distribution:

15. Common stockholders	$38 637	($0)	0.0%	$0

23

Handyware, Inc.

Handyware, Inc., has operated a chain of building supply stores in Ontario and Quebec since 1903. Until about 10 years ago, all of its stores were in older downtown locations, and its sales were to professional builders and repairers. However, in the late 1970s, the chain opened its first suburban store, which differed significantly from the older stores. The new store was much larger, stocking many more items than the old stores, which special-ordered about half the items they sold. Further, the new suburban store catered to "do-it-yourselfers" rather than to professionals.

The new concept was a resounding success, and over the past 10 years, Handyware has been aggressively selling its older locations and opening new suburban stores. The downtown areas in many of Handyware's cities have been revitalized and are now filled with high-rise office buildings and upscale retail outlets, so downtown property values have skyrocketed. Thus, the sale of its old store properties resulted in large cash inflows to Handyware. Since the company's strategic plans call for it to lease the new suburban stores rather than to purchase them, the firm now has a "war chest" of excess cash.

Many alternative uses have been discussed for the excess cash, ranging from repurchases of stock or debt to higher dividend payments. However, management has decided to use the cash to make one or more acquisitions, since they believe an expansion would contribute the most to stockholders' wealth. One of the acquisition candidates is Atlantic Hardware, a chain of 6 stores operating in eastern Canada. The issues now facing the company are (1) how to approach Atlantic's management and (2) how much to offer for Atlantic's stock.

Handyware's executives are good at running a building supply company, but they are not finance experts, and they have no experience with acquisitions. Bob Sharpe, the treasurer, has an accounting background, and last year he attended a 3-day workshop on mergers specifically to learn something about the subject. Handyware had no acquisition plans at that time, but Sharpe felt that it would be useful to become familiar with the subject.

Table 1

Incremental Cash Flows to Handyware if Atlantic is Aquired

	1991	1992	1993	1994
Net sales	$4 000 000	$6 000 000	$7 500 000	$8 500 000
Cost of goods sold (50% of sales)	2 000 000	3 000 000	3 750 000	4 250 000
Depreciation	400 000	450 000	500 000	550 000
Selling/administrative expense	300 000	400 000	500 000	600 000
Interest expense	200 000	300 000	400 000	500 000
Retentions	0	500 000	400 000	300 000

Table 1 contains some basic data that Sharpe developed relating to the cash flows Handyware could expect if it acquired Atlantic. The interest expense listed in the table includes (1) the interest on Atlantic's existing debt, (2) the interest on new debt that Handyware would issue to help finance the acquisition, and (3) the interest on new debt that Handyware would issue over time to help finance expansion within the new division. The required retentions shown in Table 1 represent earnings generated within Atlantic that would be earmarked for reinvestment within the acquired company to help finance growth. Note that the estimates in Table 1 are the end-of-year incremental flows Atlantic Hardware is expected to produce and to make available to Handyware if it is acquired by Handyware. Although specific estimates were only made for 1991 through 1994, the acquired company would be expected to grow at a 5 percent rate in 1995 and beyond.

Atlantic Hardware currently finances with 40 percent debt, it pays taxes at a 30 percent federal-plus-provincial rate, and its beta is 1.2. If the acquisition takes place, Handyware would increase Atlantic's debt ratio to 50 percent, and the consolidation of taxable income would move Atlantic's federal-plus-provincial tax rate up to that of Handyware, 40 percent.

One part of the analysis involves determining a discount rate to apply to the estimated cash flows. From the workshop he took, Sharpe remembers equations that can be used to unlever and then relever betas, and he believes that these equations may be helpful in the analysis:

Formula to unlever beta:

$$b_u = \frac{b_L}{1 + (1 - T)\,(D/S)}.$$

Formula to relever beta:

$$b_L = b_u [1 + (1 + T)\,(D/S)].$$

Here, b_u is the beta Atlantic would have if it used no debt financing, T is the applicable corporate tax rate, and D/S is the applicable market value debt-to-equity ratio. Sharpe notes that long term government of Canada Bonds are yielding 10 percent, and a call to the company's investment dealers produced an estimate of 6 percent for the market risk premium.

Assume that you were recently hired as Sharpe's assistant, and he has asked you to answer some basic questions about mergers as well as to do some calculations pertaining to the proposed Atlantic acquisition. Then, you and Sharpe will meet with the board of directors, and it will decide whether or not to proceed with the acquisition, how to start the negotiations, and the maximum price to offer. As you go through the questions, recognize that either Sharpe or anyone on the board could ask you follow-up questions, so you should thoroughly understand the implications of each question and answer. Your predecessor was fired for "being too mechanical and superficial," and you don't want to suffer the same fate.

Questions

1. Several factors have been proposed as providing a rationale for mergers. Among the more prominent are (1) tax considerations, (2) diversification, (3) control, (4) purchase of assets below replacement cost, and (5) synergy. From the standpoint of economic efficiency, which of these reasons are justifiable? Which are not? Why is such a question relevant to a company, like Handyware, that is considering a specific acquisition? Explain your answers.

2. Briefly describe the differences between a hostile merger and a friendly merger. Is there any reason to think that acquiring companies would, on average, pay a greater premium over target companies' preannouncement prices for hostile mergers than for friendly mergers?

3. Use the data contained in Table 1 to construct Atlantic's cash flow statements for 1991 through 1994. Why is interest expense typically deducted in merger cash flow statements, whereas it is not normally deducted in capital budgeting cash flow analysis? Why are retained earnings (retentions) deducted in the cash flow statements?

4. Conceptually, what is the appropriate discount rate to apply to the cash flows developed in Question 3? What is its numerical value? How much confidence can one place in this estimate; that is, is the estimated discount rate likely to be in error by a small amount, such as 1 percentage point, or a large amount, such as 4 or 5 percentage points?

5. What is the terminal value of Atlantic Hardware; that is, what is the 1994 value of the cash flows Atlantic is expected to generate beyond 1994? What is Atlantic's value to Handyware at the beginning of 1991? Suppose another firm was evaluating Atlantic as a potential acquisition candidate. Would they obtain the same value? Explain.

6. **a.** Suppose Atlantic's management has a substantial ownership interest in the company, but not enough to block a merger. If Atlantic's managers want to keep the firm independent, what are some actions they could take that might discourage potential suitors?

   b. If Atlantic's managers conclude that they cannot remain independent, what are some actions they might take to help their stockholders (and themselves) get the maximum price for their stock?

   c. If Atlantic's managers conclude that the maximum price they can get anyone to bid for the company is less than its "true value," is there any other action they might take that would benefit both outside stockholders and the managers themselves? Explain.

   d. Do Atlantic's managers face any potential conflicts of interest in any of the situations presented in parts a through c? Explain, and suggest what might be done to reduce the damage from conflicts of interest.

7. Atlantic has 5 million shares of common stock outstanding. The shares are traded infrequently and in small blocks, but the last trade, of 500 shares, was at a price of $1.50 per share. Based on this information, and on your answers to Questions 5 and 6, how much should Handyware offer, per share, for Atlantic, and how should it go about making the offer?

8. Do you agree that synergistic effects create value in the average merger? If so, how is this value generally shared between the stockholders of the acquiring and acquired companies; that is, does more of the value go to the acquired or to the acquiring firm? Explain.

9. A major concern in the analysis is the accuracy of the post-1993 growth rate; how could the maximum price vary if this rate were greater or less than the expected 5 percent? If you are using the *Lotus* model, do a sensitivity analysis designed to determine the importance of the growth rate, and determine the minimum growth rate that would justify a price of $2 per share. If you do not have access to the *Lotus* model, simply discuss the issue, and explain why managers would be interested in such a sensitivity analysis.

10. Another major concern is the discount rate used in the analysis. What would Atlantic's value to Handyware be if Atlantic's beta were higher or lower than the 1.2 originally estimated, or if the market risk premium were above or below the estimated 6 percent? Discuss the effects of these factors on the acquisition, and on the amount Handyware should offer. If you are using the *Lotus* model, quantify your results; otherwise, just discuss the issues.

11. Would the response of Atlantic's stockholders be affected by the form of payment, that is, whether the offer was for cash or for stock in Handyware? Explain.

12. What are your final conclusions regarding the amount Handyware should offer, and the form of the offer?

To the Owner of this Book:

We are interested in your reaction to *Cases in Financial Management, First Canadian Edition*. Through feedback from you, we may be able to improve this book in future editions.

1. What was your reason for using this book?

   _____ college course

   _____ university course

   _____ continuing education

   _____ other (please specify)

2. If you used this text for a program, what was the name of that program?

3. Which chapters or sections were omitted from your course?

4. Have you any suggestions for improving this text?

Fold here
- -

**Business
Reply Mail**

No Postage Stamp
Necessary if Mailed
in Canada

Canada Post / Postes Canada
43652

POSTAGE WILL BE PAID BY

SCOTT DUNCAN

EDITORIAL DIRECTOR

COLLEGE DIVISION

Holt, Rinehart and Winston
  of Canada, Limited
55 Horner Avenue
Toronto, Ontario
M8Z 9Z9